DIGITAL CUSTOMER EXPERIENCE ENGINEERING

STRATEGIES FOR CREATING EFFECTIVE DIGITAL EXPERIENCES

Lars Wiedenhoefer

Apress®

Digital Customer Experience Engineering: Strategies for Creating Effective Digital Experiences

Lars Wiedenhoefer
Austin, TX, USA

ISBN-13 (pbk): 978-1-4842-7242-8   ISBN-13 (electronic): 978-1-4842-7243-5
https://doi.org/10.1007/978-1-4842-7243-5

Managing Director, Apress Media LLC: Welmoed Spahr
Acquisitions Editor: Shiva Ramachandran
Development Editor: Matthew Moodie
Coordinating Editor: Jessica Vakili

Distributed to the book trade worldwide by Springer Science+Business Media New York, 1 New York Plaza, New York, NY 100043. Phone 1-800-SPRINGER, fax (201) 348-4505, e-mail orders-ny@springer-sbm.com, or visit www.springeronline.com. Apress Media, LLC is a California LLC and the sole member (owner) is Springer Science + Business Media Finance Inc (SSBM Finance Inc). SSBM Finance Inc is a Delaware corporation.

For information on translations, please e-mail booktranslations@springernature.com; for reprint, paperback, or audio rights, please e-mail bookpermissions@springernature.com.

Apress titles may be purchased in bulk for academic, corporate, or promotional use. eBook versions and licenses are also available for most titles. For more information, reference our Print and eBook Bulk Sales web page at http://www.apress.com/bulk-sales.

Any source code or other supplementary material referenced by the author in this book is available to readers on GitHub via the book's product page, located at www.apress.com/978-1-4842-7242-8. For more detailed information, please visit http://www.apress.com/source-code.

Printed on acid-free paper

*To all of you who care about the
digital customer experience journey.*

Contents

About the Author

Lars Wiedenhoefer is currently a Customer Experience Engineering Strategist and Program Manager at Bazaarvoice, having previously worked at companies like PayPal and Dell.

Lars is an accomplished technology leader and strategist focused on digital customer experience improvements achieved by speeding up the feedback loop through enhancing observability techniques in departments of engineering and customer technical support. Results include improved software engineering capabilities, security, speed to market, end-user experience, cost savings, and increased revenue. He has global, enterprise-level experience in various industries such as Ecommerce, FinTech, and Healthcare Tech. His areas of emphasis are strength-based organizational growth and leadership development applied to his teams and the organization, with passion for superior digital customer experiences.

Acknowledgments

Writing a book during a pandemic was certainly not on my mind. In fact, I convinced myself that writing a book was for writers, and definitely not for somebody like me. Then, one day, I talked about my customer experience passion to Pedro García, an author and personal brand strategist, and there it was. He said I needed to write a book. After initially dismissing his advice, I became curious and read Fernando Doglio's article "8 Steps to Publish Your First Technical Book" on Medium. Now I felt empowered and motivated to become a person who can write a book. Thank you for the inspiration and encouragement.

To my family who gave me the space, love, and support to write a book during a long winter in the first year of the pandemic during which we experienced unemployment, remote working, COVID itself, a harsh winter storm in Texas, and other experiences testing us seemingly on a weekly basis.

To my colleagues and mentor at PayPal. You have set up the dedication to excellence and customer experience innovation that inspired me. It resulted in making excellence in digital customer experience engineering my career pursuit.

To my colleagues at Bazaarvoice. Your energy and passion for pushing forward with customer experience excellence makes it a joy to come to work every day. Many of you are already modeling the techniques covered in this book, and some of you are authors referenced here, drivers of customer experience observability, and creative innovators. Thank you for having me as part of your team.

Introduction

Why is this book needed?

When thinking about writing a book about digital customer experience engineering, quite a few questions came to mind: "Why is a book needed?", "Who is the audience?", and of course "Is there enough value to write about?"

Let me answer the "Why" question first by going into how I detected the need and key components of this function.

When I was in the role of a manager of tech support of a major international financial services company, key parts of the role were to develop a deep understanding of the impact of issues, to understand and optimize the speed of the engineering feedback loop (issue resolution time), and to develop the ability to calculate the cost of the issues or customer friction to the business (in aggregate and on a case-by-case basis). To provide input, answers, and proactive solutions to these key topics, I had access to large amounts of operational data on the engineering, call center operations, and customer experience side.

The information I had access to provided me with the following insights:

- On average, most affected customers do not call in about an issue. In fact, only about 20%–30% do.

- The costs of resolving issues and the cost to operations add up quickly.

- The time it takes to resolve the issues (as measured from the time of detection to the resolution for all impacted customers) is substantial and noticeable for most issues.

My team of very talented support engineers became adept at meeting these challenges head on and, over the years, getting into a proactive stance, developing insights and techniques that allowed us to meet these challenges by

- Increasing observability to include customers who are impacted but do not call in, affording them a voice in the resolution of their issue

- Saving significant money and adding additional revenue by addressing customer friction proactively in collaboration with product, engineering, and SRE (Site Reliability Engineering) functions

- Reducing the average time of an issue resolution by 81%

The cross-functional leadership and mentoring skills as well as the engineering techniques learned from this proactive stance are quite valuable and teachable and provide the reason for why it is important to compile them into a book.

Having since worked with other technology organizations in FinTech, Ecommerce, and even MedTech, patterns of applicability emerged that proved each time how applicable these techniques are and how uplifting an experience it was for the teams, departments, and organizations that deployed them.

The uplift was experienced by engineers as they experienced a higher degree of empathy with the customer as they were in touch with them even prior to delivery of their features and product increments. The engineers created meaningful insights and data points that allowed the feedback loop to be optimized to the point that the efficiencies gained saved the company money as it also earned the company a higher Net Promoter Score (NPS) with their customers.

Whenever my teams and engineers worked with others in a proactive stance to address issues of speeding up the feedback loop, we educated and taught as many other engineers as we could. There were many who learned and picked up the techniques.

So, why is this book needed? The purpose of this book is to express the learnings and insights gained from the development of a proactive stance toward a product-centric engineering discipline that I call "digital customer experience engineering."

As the audience for this book, I am generally trying to address anybody who is participating in the value stream of digital software engineering for the benefit of customer experiences, directly or indirectly. You may be an engineer practicing DevOps or site reliability, or you might be a product owner, UX designer, or researcher. And you might be working in support and seeking for new ways to engage with your engineering teams. I believe there are valuable points for each of you in this book.

Of course, this leads to the tougher question: "Is there enough value to write about?"

Let me answer in this way: There is enough value in this book if you are empathetic with your customers and desire for them to have great experiences. And there is even more value in this book if you are in a job role in the product or engineering departments of your company.

This book will discuss how to gain customer insights faster and through new and insightful sources, elegantly linked and within your reach. It will teach you to anticipate your customers' needs and to react as quickly as your customers would expect.

With these skills in place, your team, organization, or company will gain a competitive edge over the competition. In my experience, I have seen the benefits to happier employees, higher job satisfaction levels, faster and more reliable innovative releases, and happier customers by multiple verifiable measures.

The Importance of Acting Today

Getting digital experiences right is not optional

Before getting started and taking action, a clear understanding of the definition of digital customer experience is needed. This chapter will provide a clear definition, will look at the top three challenges to overcome, and outline the return on investment that can be expected as a motivation to get started today.

The Business Drivers

Before going through the business drivers of digital customer experience, it might be a good idea to look into defining the concept of customer experience itself as a starting point.

Customer experience is defined as

> the internal and subjective response customers have to any direct or indirect contact with a company.

> —Andre Schwager and Chris Meyer,
> "Understanding Customer Experience"

© Lars Wiedenhoefer 2021
L. Wiedenhoefer, *Digital Customer Experience Engineering*,
https://doi.org/10.1007/978-1-4842-7243-5_1

A **digital customer experience** is therefore an internal and subjective response of the customer to a digital product the customer interacts with, typically an app on their smart device or a website. Now, the 21st-century digital customer has high expectations: they like their experience to be quick, up to the task, straight to the point, pleasant, and without friction. If such positive experiences are not offered, they are quick to turn to competitors.

Focusing on the digital customer experience means keeping your customers happy and engaged. And investing in customer experience is not only necessary but paramount.

According to a study by the Temkin Group, SaaS (Software as a Service) companies double their revenue within 36 months. In fact, they found that a $1 billion investment yields the same amount within three years.

With such a strong financial opportunity incentive, the question might come up if there are perhaps other obstacles to enter this field. In an article, Qualtrics XM provides a possible answer:

> *69% of companies say the biggest challenge to a differentiated customer experience is designing and managing cross-channel experiences.*
>
> —Jack Davies, "Customer journeys are more complex than ever. Understanding them doesn't have to be."

Top Three Challenges to Overcome

Per Jack Davies' article, the top three challenges for improving the customer experience can be described as

1. Data silos containing different and unrelated customer data spread across the organization

2. Lack of integration of customer data and listening across a dynamic omnichannel customer journey

3. Creating an aligned culture of employee empowerment and organizational action to adjust to the dynamic nature of the customer journey

---

■ **Note**   This book aims to help the reader in overcoming these three central challenges.

In regard to data silos, the book will provide guidance on how to make the data accessible. Organizations are keeping track of an abundance of useful technical and tracing data, which are typically anonymized, yet quite useful when linked together while keeping the privacy of their users intact.

The book will discuss ways to gain useful customer experience insights from such siloed data and will discuss where to find them. This approach will also address concern number two in the preceding list while focusing on the digital channels in play.

The third point will be addressed by identifying the need of a function dedicated to overcoming the digital customer experience challenges and how this function interacts with other functions in the organization.

This book aims to provide you, the reader, with a framework of how to overcome the typical business and technical challenges with relative ease while unlocking the opportunity to reap the financial rewards of creating delightful customer experiences.

Opportunities

Optimize the structure of the traditional digital engineering feedback loop

Awareness of the traditional software development life cycle is important in order to understand the feedback loop and the need to optimize it for optimal digital customer experiences.

What is a feedback loop? In this book, the term refers to the feedback provided during the software development life cycle regarding quality and fitness for purpose, including the feedback provided by customers after digital experiences and features are released.

In this chapter, we will look closer at the opportunities for optimization as a preparation for the other chapters in this book.

Insights into the Traditional Digital Software Engineering Feedback Loop

Modern software engineering teams are typically agile in nature and release their software in subsequent continuous releases. Before they release anything, they typically go through rigorous steps of designing, developing, and testing the experience. They go through great lengths to ensure that they built the

L. Wiedenhoefer, *Digital Customer Experience Engineering*,
https://doi.org/10.1007/978-1-4842-7243-5_2

experience right, meaning free of software "bugs," with sound engineering underpinnings for maximum uptime and availability.

After such releases, there is naturally a continuous feedback loop, as depicted in Figure 2-1, providing feedback on their experiences with the new features in previous releases and their envisioned benefits. This feedback either comes back in direct form or indirect form.

The direct form could include calls to a support hotline, emails to a support inbox, or feedback via live chat or could be embedded in product ratings and reviews.

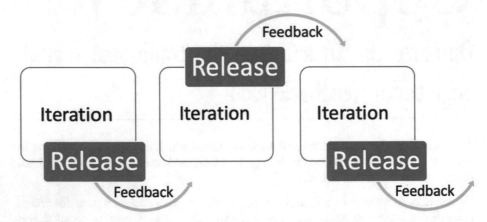

Figure 2-1. Illustration of the feedback loop

The indirect feedback, which occurs way more often, is more subliminal and includes frustrated, but silent, users trying to find workarounds, clicking in frustration, are baffled, or simply just walk away. If the nature of the feedback is anything but positive, there are naturally undesired negative side effects to a business releasing such features. And if this occurs, the engineering team that released such an increment to the product just didn't meet the need of the customer, in fact, they didn't build the right product as it didn't delight the customer and wasn't without friction or even created confusion with the customer.

Now, in an ideal world, it would be optimal if the teams releasing the software had the ability to observe any kind of issues with their software immediately after the release so that they could effectively course-correct and fix the issue. Such a feedback loop would be ideal as the releasing team, in this scenario, has the maximum degree of observability to their disposal through which they detect and fix issues that are easy for them to fix as they are still close to the context of their previous work and the subsequent release of the features involved in the release.

While such an ideal scenario is increasingly more possible through ever-improving observability tools and techniques, the normal feedback scenario is less immediate. Software engineering teams are often structured in a way where they are organizationally removed from the customer feedback collection mechanism. They are reporting into the engineering organization, which is separated from the support, client success, customer experience (CX), or user experience (UX) teams. In a traditional organization, the engineers are dependent on customer escalations coming their way through "bugs," which they will then prioritize and work on. Additionally, an organization might collect NPS scores and receive feedback through UX research. To an engineering team, the NPS numbers are quite abstract and not immediately actionable. UX research and even customer journey maps are seldom discussed at a level where engineers can utilize them as a mechanism to accelerate their feedback loop through better visibility.

The issue with this scenario should be obvious: by the time any meaningful feedback reaches the team, they have already moved on, and the issues presented to them are not in the context of their work that led to the "bug" or issue report in the first place. Hence, they have to spend extra time to identify and remedy the root cause of the issue. Any time spent on the root cause analysis in conjunction with fixing the issue takes away from the team's ability to release innovative net new incremental business value. In other words, it slows down the team and, in most cases, provides an environment of agony and drudgery any good engineer is willing to work hard for to avoid.

A Framework of Opportunities Making the Feedback Loop More Efficient

To address these issues, that is, to speed up the feedback loop, the engineering team needs to be allowed to invest into techniques providing them the maximum degree of observability of customer experience issues when and as they occur, not too much later. And when they are aware of customer experience friction of any kind, they need to be empowered by processes, internal collaboration, and modern tools to quickly get to the root cause of the issue and get the customer experience friction fixed.

Multiple opportunities of friction detection and acceleration are going to be discussed in this book. The changes needed are quite subtle, yet decisive. Once teams are aware of the opportunities and how to unlock them, there is no turning back anymore. The benefits to them, the organization, and ultimately to the customer are just too large to pass up.

To summarize, the acceleration opportunities in the traditional feedback loop could be realized via the following framework of actions:

- Create observability into the experiences of customers for team members who are not directly interacting via support.

- Accelerate the recognition of customer sentiment by the engineering and product teams that are typically hidden within the support queues.

- Develop an early detection mechanism and framework for customer experience–related friction associated to software issues (note: issues here do not only include "bugs" and errors; the notion is wider in scope and contains any friction the customer might experience with the software and their digital customer journey).

Prior to illustrating how to address these opportunities and convert them into reality, the following chapters will provide the needed definition of the discipline involved and will outline the interactions with other disciplines.

Digital Customer Experience Engineering

A discipline envisioned

As we understand the opportunities to optimize the feedback loop from the prior chapter, we now need a closer look into the techniques that are needed to shorten the feedback loop to quickly respond to customer friction elements in the digital experience.

In this chapter, we will define a new discipline, digital customer experience engineering. We will look at why there is a need for the role and understand how the digital customer experience engineer accelerates the feedback loop via the acceleration cycle. For engineers interested in how this role would fit into their software engineering value creation pipeline, we will review how digital customer experience engineering looks at the software delivery pipeline from the first commit to the release of a software experience or feature.

© Lars Wiedenhoefer 2021
L. Wiedenhoefer, *Digital Customer Experience Engineering*,
https://doi.org/10.1007/978-1-4842-7243-5_3

The Definition

With the enhanced focus on digital experiences, it is time to introduce a new discipline or at least a new perspective that provides engineering teams with the visibility and observability they need to speed up the software engineering feedback loop and to drive to meaningful innovations faster, with less pain and more delight.

Customer experience engineering is about pulling from various disciplines and introducing principles and tools to fortify a method of gathering valuable insights that have the power to accelerate and ease the creation of the optimal incremental value released by the respective software engineering team. These methods are applied pre-release, at the point of release, and, naturally, after the release. It's the special insights gathered after release and the way they inform the software development process that's fundamentally modern.

Let's take a look at the definition.

Digital customer experience engineering (DCXE) as a discipline seeks to optimize all processes within the software engineering craft involved in the creation of digital experiences and digital customer experience journeys with the goal of crafting and establishing experience observability into customer interactions with the digital product.

■ **Note**   The abbreviation **DCXE** will be used throughout the book to describe either the discipline digital customer experience engineering or the engineer(s) performing the work as in digital customer experience engineer(s).

The digital customer experience engineer (DCXE) starts with the desired customer experience outcome in mind and creates a measuring mechanism allowing the verification and validation of the experience outcomes, thus creating observability. The engineer starts with a hypothesis of the desired outcome and works to verify the assumptions. The engineer is guided by observations into the experiences and behavior of the customers as an aggregate, looking for issues within the journey such as friction, confusion, or simply a drop-off.

Insights gained from such measurements are utilized to monitor the customer experience at the time of the release of a new feature or experience and throughout the experience's life cycle (from further refinements to eventual decommission). The engineer, in conjunction with the team responsible for the digital experience, aims to perpetually refine the measurements toward gaining an optimal number of insights into possible customer experience friction. Utilizing such insights, the engineer works with multiple teams to fortify and strengthen the software delivery pipeline. The digital customer experience engineer works with the product team and other engineers to seek for changes in the delivery pipeline in order to eradicate the root cause of customer experience friction. Such friction could be caused by behaviors along the CI/CD (Continuous Integration/Continuous Delivery) pipeline or might be rooted in the architecture or environments utilized to build the experience.

Figure 3-1 shows the disciplines the digital customer experience engineer interacts with most often. More details into interactions with these functions and others will be devoted in Chapter 5.

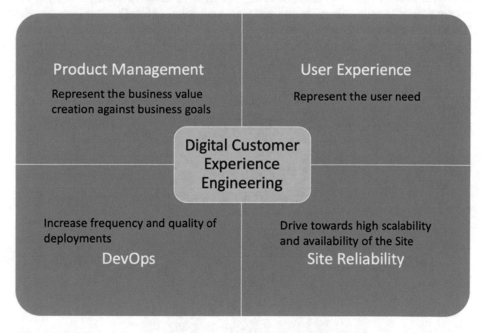

Figure 3-1. Digital customer experience engineering as a central practice connecting other disciplines

At this point, it is important to highlight that the DCXE works closely with the user experience (UX) team to obtain a model of the desired customer experience journey. The digital customer experience engineer works with product management to understand the desired customer experience requirements going into an agile development iteration. The digital customer experience engineer crafts release success criteria (e.g., funnel, engagement, or retention goals) and works along with the engineering team to build the measurements into the observability tools prior to release. At and after release, the customer experience engineer monitors the success criteria and alerts the product team of any deviations that could point to friction, negation of the customer success, or negation of the desired business value of the new iteration.

Form, Function, and Communication

In most organizations producing a product, there are groups in that organization representing the form of the product, while others represent the function. Both are coordinated by leadership in the goal toward the product vision and are supported by a collaborative culture.

Figure 3-2 illustrates the concept of the interplay between communication, form, and function. Communication is typically represented by leadership setting the tone via the organization's vision and the culture. Form is typically represented by the product, marketing, and sales organizations, whereas groups like engineering, architecture, and site reliability represent the functional element of the product. Together they are collaborating on the optimal outcome and alignment: a product resonating well with the market for continued business success.

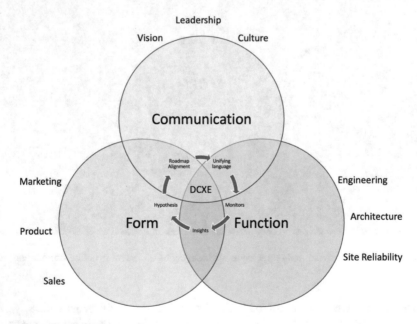

Figure 3-2. The DCXE acceleration cycle

While collaborating on working toward the optimal product and the introduction of new features, the groups representing form, function, and communication grow closer together, as represented by the Venn diagram in Figure 3-2.

The idea of the DCXE function is based on the observation that positive forces advocating for the optimal customer benefits can be beneficial to the entire organization by working on accelerating factors that bring the groups together faster and bond them together in a more enduring way.

The accelerating forces the DCXE function contributes are illustrated in Figure 3-2. The concepts are touched on in the following in a brief fashion. A detailed discussion of the work done by the DCXE function will follow in a later chapter.

Hypothesis

The term hypothesis represents the bet that's being made by conceiving and commissioning the rollout of a new product or feature. The DCXE works on identifying ways to describe the critical success parameters of the product or feature into measurable customer centric success criteria.

Unifying Language

In some organizations, groups representing the form of the product or feature describe it differently than groups representing the function. This leads to miscommunication and confusion that is detectable during the entire product development life cycle. The DCXE helps to bridge the communication gaps by introducing a common language illustrating form, function, and the successful application of both in the product or feature. The common language is represented by the consistent naming of key elements within the customer journey, user interactions, feedback events, engagement parameters, as well as qualitative measures such as notions of adoption, lack of friction, clarity and ease of the customer's interaction with the product and feature. The benefits of such a common language are resulting in a stronger partnership between groups representing form and function.

Monitors

The DCXE crafts customer- and product-centric monitors that allow the development and product teams to observe the success criteria representing the optimal and frictionless customer interactions. Keep in mind that the product development team already described the acceptance criteria that defined how to measure that the product was built right (technically sound). The customer experience monitors extend the acceptance criteria by adding observability measures aimed at measuring if the team built the right product for the customer. The monitors are very relevant as soon as the product or feature transitions into production. At that moment, the teams responsible for the product or feature need to have ways to observe customer success closely, represented by the modeling of the success criteria via monitors (e.g., customer journey funnel representations, friction heatmaps, engagement and retention measures).

Insights

The DCXE increases the capacity of the software development team to gain an accurate, deep, and exceedingly intuitive understanding of the product experience in the form of insights gained from the developed and deployed monitors. Insights into the adoption, the flow of interactions, interaction success, and other measures are very valuable in determining success quickly after the release. The insights guide the direction toward an exceedingly more pleasant user experience. They are not only forward looking in nature, aiming to remove friction for future rollouts, but also protective in nature as such insights aim to detect and prevent regressions.

Road Map Alignment

The DCXE helps with alignment in various ways. In general terms, alignment here means providing focus on what matters most: customer experience–enhancing measures. The DCXE represents a way to determine the impact of certain design or engineering decisions through establishing customer experience monitors and measures.

The alignment concept might become clearer in the question most software development teams ask: how much test coverage do we need? Some teams like to say they are driving toward a certain percentage of coverage. But then they quickly start further discussions into the coverage of what: code coverage or line coverage? The DCXE volunteers the idea to focus on the discussion regarding the representation of the monitors and measurements that were established to measure user interaction flow, success, and retention. The DCXE will advise the team to provide the coverage of test cases aligned with the customer experience monitors and measurements so that they can gain optimal coverage and reuse the measurements for the determination of load and performance test flows as well as release success. Contributing to this discussion is the ability of the DCXE to advise what kind of test data should be created pre-production, as the DCXE represents the digital modeling of the customer (the personas or customer segments).

Digital Customer Experience Engineering CI/CD Pipeline Touchpoints

Figures 3-3 and 3-4 illustrate a left-to-right view of a typical software engineering delivery pipeline enhanced with elements contributed by the discipline of digital customer experience engineering. A high degree of sophisticated automation, integration of tools and visualization of quality gates aid the engineering team in maintaining code and functional excellence.

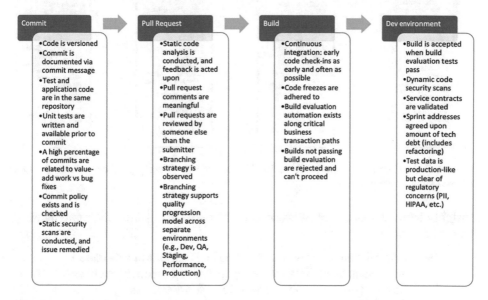

Figure 3-3. Customer experience focus throughout the delivery pipeline – from commit to the development environment

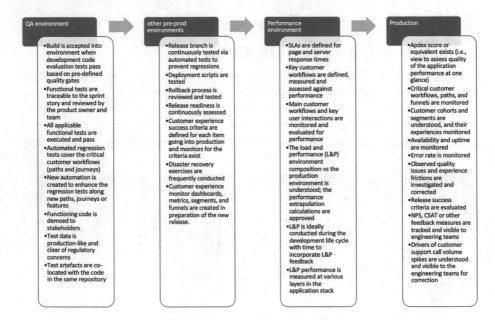

Figure 3-4. Customer experience focus throughout the delivery pipeline – from the QA environment to production

Insights from customer observations (shift right) are gained by implementing the following:

- Critical customer workflows and interactions are modeled and monitored. The modeling includes customer journey flows (success or conversion funnels), as well as engagement and retention measures.

- The error rate is measured and correlated to the overall customer experience. Are errors helpful or are they a nuisance that confuse or irritate the customer? The root causes for nuisance errors are captured and fixed.

- The engineering team has access to customer feedback provided to customer support or customer success teams. The engineering team discusses the customer feedback with the product owner for prevention strategies that might include changes to the product, additional A/B tests, or monitors to study the feedback more.

Insights from customer observations are propagated into the software delivery cycle early (shift left) by adopting the following:

- Customer experience success criteria are defined for each item going into production. Success criteria include the customer experience measures released for the item and how they will be monitored.

- The testing strategy, including load and performance tests, and the associated test data are informed by customer experience flows and engagement. For example, all the regression flows tested in a QA or staging environment have complete coverage of all essential customer journey flows in production and mimic their data throughput. Similarly, the load and performance test scenarios are analogous to the main customer journey flows.

- Functional tests are constructed based on customer experience observation. For new functionality, tests are initially constructed based on hypothetical customer experience. After the release of the functionality, real-world customer behavior and customer experience are taken into account when tests are evaluated against the pre-release hypothesis. They might have to be redesigned to cover real customer behavior flows. Adopting this adjustment behavior of tests after every release will yield a regression test repository that's evergreen and in tune with the customers.

- Build validation tests include key customer functionality. It's recommended to include all items that drive high customer engagement. From experience, this typically includes less than 20% of all the features of a product.

- Customer experience monitoring activities are planned for each iteration and given the priority they deserve.

Teams implementing key insights from customer experience observations (shift-right posture) early on into their delivery pipeline (shift-left posture) will gain multiple benefits:

- Less rework
- Less reported issues after release
- A quicker generation and validation of customer value

- Stronger data points contributing to meaningful discussions with the product and user experience teams

- A higher issue signal-to-noise ratio, meaning signals indicating issues in the delivery pipeline are indicating meaningful customer issues and are not perceived as nuisance noise

Please note that Figure 3-3 is not meant to be exhaustive and all-encompassing. It is meant as a starting point and a guiding map for tailoring to any specific engineering team's respective purpose. The chart may look slightly different if they are focused on front-end UI work or engaged in middleware, platform, or other underlying or underpinning layers of the technology stack.

The Goals

And guiding principles

As we are introducing a new discipline, digital customer experience engineering, guidance for the discipline and discipline-specific goals are essential for the practitioners to succeed in their mission toward digital customer experience excellence. In this chapter, we will review the goals, guiding principles, as well as how the discipline meets business and engineering goals.

Combining Engineering and Business Goals

The goal of the discipline of digital customer experience engineering is to build bridges between disciplines with the goal of increasing the observability of customer experience issues earlier in the product life cycle. Through deeper insights gained from establishing quantitative and qualitative observability, the engineering team is enabled via the craft of the digital customer experience engineer to empathize with their customer, hear their voice, and act toward improving the digital experiences under their control. The engineering team validates business value assumptions through data and insights and collaborates with product managers and product owners as well as user experience researchers and designers in the goal to convert customer quality into business success.

© Lars Wiedenhoefer 2021
L. Wiedenhoefer, *Digital Customer Experience Engineering*,
https://doi.org/10.1007/978-1-4842-7243-5_4

In recent years, "shift left" seems to be the answer to improving quality. And "shift left" means to perform quality assurance–related activities as early in the life cycle of software engineering as possible. If you imagine the conception of an idea and the beginning of coding on the left side of a timeline and the release of the coded product on the right side, the idea of "shift left" starts to make sense: look at quality early and often. This makes perfect sense as it is a good practice to ensure the product is built right, meaning it's the foundation of quality within the engineering craft.

Digital customer experience engineering adds the idea of "shift right" first, before "shift left" is to be applied. "Shift right," in this context, means to do everything necessary to understand your customer well. "Shift right" contains the idea to quantitatively and qualitatively build a model and understanding of what makes a good product and experience. The digital customer experience engineer brings this focus to the engineering team enabling them to "shift right" and "shift left" while building their product. The addition of "shift-right" behavior enables them to also ascertain that they build the right product, not only that they build the product right. Great customer experiences are built by teams knowing that their product is crafted well and resonates well with the intended audience. It creates trust, engineering confidence, and, through customer loyalty, business success.

What This Is – In Less Than Six Words

A career coach asked me once to summarize in less than six words to explain what I am so passionate about when I talked about digital customer experience engineering. There are three summaries I came up with:

- Speed up the feedback cycle
- Shift right, then shift left
- Connect engineering to customer success

These concepts are quite easy to read and memorize, but not always easy to implement. There is a clear path to success though, which we will cover in a later chapter in the book.

Guiding Principles

Each discipline has guiding principles. It's the same with digital customer experience engineering. The set of guiding principles make digital customer experience engineering possible and desirable as a discipline. They also aid in inspiring the engineers involved in the discipline.

Let's have a look at the guiding principles for digital customer experience engineering.

Digital Customer Experience Observability Is Tangible and Essential

Now, more than ever, there are tools and techniques available allowing each member of a product team to benefit from digital customer experience engineering insights. These insights are quantitative and qualitative in nature. And, best of all, they do not necessitate the customer benefiting from the insights to do anything. Their interactions and experience are the guiding North Star for the digital customer experience engineer.

Observability Data Needs to Be Organized to Separate "Noise" from "Signal"

Operational data is plentiful, digital tools log a good amount of data, and tools reporting on issues are quite noisy. The noise is sometimes so "loud" that engineers have to ignore items because of noise fatigue. The digital customer experience engineer is passionate about fighting noise fatigue by collecting and bundling information that is meaningful and contributing to the report on customer experience issues and their impact.

Connecting Others to Insights Is Key

The digital customer experience engineer is an ambassador of insights, who not only creates the observability that leads to insights but also connects others in their team and organization to these valuable insights on behalf of the customer.

The DCXE is passionate about these insights. They know that once discovered they lead to business success and customer delight. They are restless in finding the insights as a way to improve their engineering practice and the software engineering craft for a smoother delivery cycle.

Dedication to Constant Investigation Toward Friction Removal

After crafting the analytical methods that generate insights, the DCXE will find that they are typically still hidden in plain sight. The insights are there but don't jump out at the engineer. Some methods and techniques need to be employed to uncover the valuable insights. The methods point to areas of investigation, and these areas are in need of inspection. Time needs to be dedicated to prospecting and unearthing of the insights. Close inspection will identify the valuable points of insights that improve customer experience. Subsequently, a quantification of impact will help prioritize the discovered insights, and teams can devote time to convert insights to positive action.

So, in short, the DCXE needs to develop rhythms that fit into the delivery rhythms of their software engineering team. Time needs to be dedicated during each delivery cycle for this kind of work.

Interactions

With adjacent functions

As illustrated in Chapter 3, the digital customer experience engineer (DCXE) does not work alone on enhancing the digital customer experience. In fact, the DCXE is a connector and in the middle of an overlapping Venn diagram of multiple interacting roles.

In this chapter, we are looking closer into whom the DCXE should work with and how. Please remember that this is not an exhaustive list. Also note that not every company has exactly the same roles. The following list is a suggestion of collaboration and can help the DCXE or someone wanting to grow into such a role set up the right communication patterns.

Stakeholder Communication

Active stakeholder communication is key as the DCXE is empowered by their qualitative and quantitative insights, which need to be shared and discussed with their network of adjacent functions. The DCXE shares their insights, feedback, and concerns on behalf of the customer. Figure 5-1 depicts the communication paths discussed within this chapter.

© Lars Wiedenhoefer 2021
L. Wiedenhoefer, *Digital Customer Experience Engineering*,
https://doi.org/10.1007/978-1-4842-7243-5_5

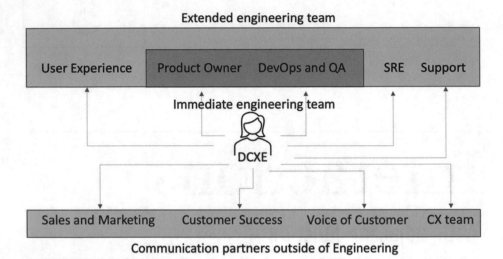

Figure 5-1. DCXE communication paths

Essential Stakeholders

The following paragraphs discuss roles that are, at a minimum, essential to the DCXE's network. They are essential stakeholders and/or input providers and partners in the journey toward a better customer experience.

The Agile Product Manager and Product Owner

The product manager and product owner represent the product road map and the customer to the team implementing the product and its features. In the development life cycle, they are essential for providing the team with the hypothesis or product idea. The development team implements the product with sound engineering practices and invests time in proving that they did their best to build the product in the right way. The DCXE needs to collaborate with the product manager and product owner to define the success criteria by which the product team will measure that the right product was built. The elements within the success criteria, represented by the DCXE on behalf of the customer, are the qualitative and quantitative measurements. We will discuss them in more detail in the metrics section of the book. On a summary level, the DCXE will discuss, after reviewing the requirements and use cases, what kind of workflows and interactions are expected. The more refined these experiences are outlined, the better.

As product teams refine their epics or stories with which they document the implementation of their product iteration, the DCXE will contribute the customer-specific success criteria of funnel flow success rates, expected engagement with the new feature, and customer retention rates. The DCXE will also outline how customer friction is qualitatively measured. This measurement will represent design problems and other friction elements that have the potential to confuse or frustrate the customer.

In summary, the product manager and owner represent the business idea or hypothesis the software development team is to implement. The DCXE works to implement measures that validate the hypothesis at release and in production via customer experience observability measures. These types of measures are called success criteria. They determine whether or not the software development team implemented the right product. There are other measures earlier in the software development life cycle that determine if the product was built right. They are typically mentioned in the acceptance criteria.

UX Team

User experience (UX) researchers and designers work on understanding user needs and evaluate design concepts, from prototype to the final product. They aim to establish processes that turn out products providing meaningful and relevant experiences to customers. Their work is done through user research, market analysis, ideation, prototyping, interviewing, and testing. They are applying methodologies to ensure a great customer experience at every step of the customer journey.

The DCXE works with the UX team to learn more about the overall product experience strategy. Such a strategy might contain aspects of the product's design and the design consistency, the approach to prototyping, the product review process, considerations around internationalization, and other important customer experience–centric elements. Most importantly, the strategy should also include a reference to the product's personas. As personas are a representation of the product's target audience, it is important for the DCXE to familiarize themselves with the personas and how they are grouped into cohorts. For anybody not familiar with the concept of personas, read the article "The ultimate guide to creating personas and how to use them to enhance your business."[1]

In summary, the DCXE receives at least three valuable takeaways from the collaboration with the UX team:

- The product experience strategy
- Journey maps and paths
- Personas

---

[1]Ergonomia UX on Medium.com, 2019

CX Team

Most companies have a customer experience (CX) team in some form:

> *Smaller businesses tend to have one person, if they have anyone at all. Mid-sized businesses tend to have at least one person, maybe up to three or five. And larger businesses go so far as to have "Office of the Customer" and much larger teams.*

> —Dom Nicastro, "What Do Customer Experience Teams Actually Look Like?"

It is paramount for the DCXE to ask around and find the individuals associated with this function. They typically represent the Voice of the Customer (VoC). Through the VoC program or other insights, the CX team can share invaluable information regarding customer feedback and sentiment.

The DCXE works to collect such feedback and tries to map it to the applicable software function that might be representing the root cause of the feedback. If the feedback is positive, the DCXE ensures the software development team knows how to protect the positive experience through prevention of regressions. If the feedback is negative, the DCXE works on identifying the associated customer path or journey and looks into working with the software development team to remove and prevent such friction in the future.

DevOps and QA

QA World describes the role of QA in the modern DevOps team. The key takeaways from their article in relation to the role of the DCXE are

> *The aim of DevOps is for teams to work collaboratively throughout, which ultimately brings greater customer satisfaction through faster turn around.*

> *In DevOps, the modern tester needs to broaden their horizon from restricting their role to bug finding, to now participating in technical meetings, contributing towards deployment, quick fixes, critical analysis, and the final review.*

> —QA World, "Is QA still relevant in DevOps? – An Introduction to DevOps Testing"

The DCXE is either a role that consults with the DevOps team or a role evolving inside of the DevOps team where typically the QA "broaden their horizon" by adding the DCXE skills of creating customer experience observability. The DCXE helps the DevOps team to identify customer experience friction points and work on improving their TTR (time to resolution) by improving RCA (root cause analysis) and accelerating the DevOps innovation value stream through removing bottlenecks in the CI/CD (Continuous Integration/Continuous Delivery) pipeline.

The DevOps practice of continuously "build, deliver, and operate" can be illustrated via an infinite loop as in Figure 5-2. It divides the loop into three segments of activities pre-release, at release, and post-release.

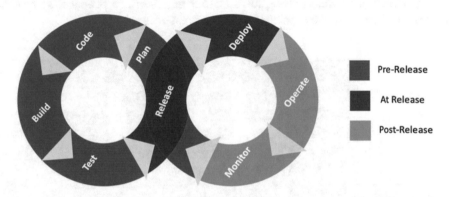

Figure 5-2. Continuous loop seen in three phases

The mental separation in three phases allows then the illustration of quality focus within these three stages (pre-release, at release, post-release) along with different dimensions or focus areas of quality going across these stages (see Figure 5-3).

> ■ **Note**   The collection of dimensions of quality is not meant to be exhaustive. There are certainly more, and it is recommended that the DCXE have a conversation within the engineering and product organizations to see what dimensions are the areas of focus for the company.

As the DCXE's focus area is observability within the engineering practice, Figure 5-3 illustrates the span of observability across the post-release activities. This does not mean that the DCXE is primarily active post-release. The DCXE works pre-release alongside all other engineers to prepare for release success and customer experience success measures.

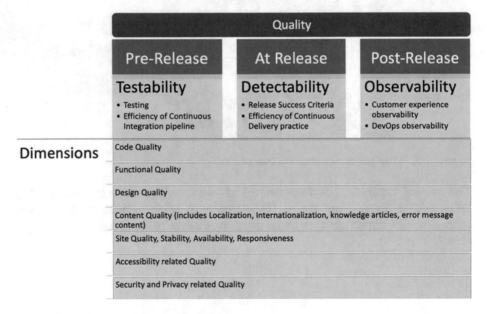

Figure 5-3. *Stages and dimensions of quality*

The DCXE's primary focus pre-release is to represent the Voice of the Customer during pre-release activities by working with the quality engineers working on software testing.

At the time of release, the DCXE focuses on ensuring the measures for the release success criteria are in place. See the section "Implement the Idea of Success Criteria" in Chapter 6 for details on success criteria.

After the release of a software feature, the DCXE's focus is to represent the customer experience observability across all of the dimensions of quality while working closely with the team members focused on DevOps observability and Site Reliability Engineering.

For a definition of what's meant here by "DevOps observability," let's turn to Google:

> *Observability is tooling or a technical solution that allows teams to actively debug their system. Observability is based on exploring properties and patterns not defined in advance.*

—Google, *Site Reliability Engineering*

The DCXE works with the DevOps engineers to align the customer observability platform and measures with the DevOps observability platform. The customer observability platform focuses on customer experience issues and friction points, whereas the focus of the DevOps observability platform is centered around tracing, diagnosing, and understanding production infrastructure and environment issues. These infrastructure and production environment issues can be linked to customer issues and friction points. This is why a close collaboration and alignment of these observability techniques is required.

Support Team

The DCXE can help the support team by showing how better observability has a positive effect on supportability improvements. In fact, from my own experience, it shows that even small investments into customer experience tooling and training of a few key engineers pay off within the same year.

Think of the following business case. There are times where a support team has to ask the customer for supporting information for the case under investigation in the form of logs (e.g., HAR logs or the browser source code via the developer tab). I've experienced this personally within two different multinational organizations. This is not only embarrassing but also time-consuming and quite frustrating for the support personnel and the customer. A customer experience observability tool easily addresses this issue by eradicating the need to ask the customer such an embarrassing and labor-intensive question.

Let's look at a business case illustrating how much money could be saved by implementing a DCXE function in this space.

If there's a tool that allows the support team to identify the customers' actions and retrace them, this shaves off at least one hour from the support cases on average, as multiple people work on the cases, and each person is trying to retrace the steps taken. Let's say there are 80 applicable support cases in the queue per week. Furthermore, let's assume the loaded labor cost for the hour is $70. Per week, just by asking for additional log information, the cost setback is $80 \times \$70 = \$5600$. With 52 weeks in a year, this one question costs your department already $291,200 per year. A starting investment into observability tools is much less. The benefits of such an investment are clear: quicker support time, happier customers as they are not overburdened with providing proof of their issue, happier support engineers as they are getting to the root cause of the issue quicker, and a positive return as money is saved as well.

There is even more a DCXE can do in conjunction with the support team. The DCXE should get insight into the support queue or queues for products or customers. It is important for the DCXE to take the sentiment submitted by customers via the support tickets into account for their observability strategy and analysis. The DCXE should create reports by product from multiple perspectives:

- Incoming tickets into the Salesforce or Zendesk CRM queue (or whichever CRM your organization uses)

- Escalated support tickets to the technical teams (can be measured via JIRA or any other bug reporting tool you are using as customer experience bugs)

- Issue tickets due to outages (any form of degraded performance impacting uptime and availability)

From here, the DCXE identifies key bottlenecks and works with the teams involved to come up with proactive mitigation strategies. It is also recommended to measure the time to resolution for any customer-impacting issues. The DCXE identifies engineering friction points that slow down the root cause analysis and advocates for engineering friction removal while providing assistance in establishing visibility into issue traceability.

Results of these activities lead to a faster feedback cycle, less recurring issues over time, and a general increased organizational awareness of customer experience issues.

Site Reliability Engineering (SRE)

SRE is what you get when you treat operations as if it's a software problem.

—Google, *Site Reliability Engineering*

SRE cares about creating and maintaining reliable systems with a maximum possible system uptime and availability. And as such, they are driven by reducing failures as quickly as possible and are conscientious of the cost of failures. As they are treating operations as a software problem, they are naturally driven to increase observability into system issues. This is done in a very prescriptive way by establishing Service Level Indicators (SLIs) and Service Level Objectives (SLOs). Both SLIs and SLOs are very customer experience–centric measures and thus the ideal touchpoint with the DCXE, as the DCXE specifically drives toward the best possible service levels for optimal customer experiences. The SLOs expand on the SLIs by setting service-level goals over time. SLIs establish, for example, the availability of a system as a key measure. For example, all responses are received by the customer within two seconds. The availability Service Level Objective might be to have an availability goal of 99.97% of the time, which means that 99.97% of the time the SLI of 100% response within two seconds is true.

The DCXE works with the SRE team to craft SLIs and SLOs from a customer-centric view and assist with the drive toward speeding up the feedback loop by shortening the TTR (time to restore) period when failures occur. Both do this via intelligent measures and software engineering practices. The DCXE is focused on the detection and classification of the issues and the removal of software issues within a function or feature. The SRE function ensures the site that's serving the function or feature is stable and available.

Together, the DCXE and SRE engineers are collaborating in understanding which signals impact the site and the ability to service the customer experience. The section "Increasing the Signal-to-Noise Ratio of Alerting Tools" in Chapter 6 explains the involvement of the DCXE further.

Customer Success Team

> *Customer success teams are dedicated to helping customers achieve their goals.*
>
> —Blake Toder, "8 Steps to Building a Strong Customer Success Team"

As customer success teams are assisting customers, they typically capture the customer inquiries in the form of customer support tickets or contact notes.

In order to improve the overall customer experience, the customer success team might collect additional information in the form of reviews regarding the customers' product experience. Such reviews might include the Net Promoter Score (NPS) as a key metric.

The metric NPS is defined as

> *% Promoters - % Detractors = NPS (Net Promoter Score)*
>
> —NICE Satmetrix, "What Is Net Promoter?"

Promoters are typically the scores nine and ten on a scale of zero to ten. Passives are the scores seven and eight. They are satisfied customers, but just not promoters. Detractors are customers rating the product or experience zero to six. They are quite unhappy and will use negative word of mouth, which can be damaging for a brand.

The DCXE should be interested in learning about customer sentiment through the contact notes and the NPS reviews and results. Information from these sources should be used to enhance observability into customer friction points, their early detection, and mitigation.

Customer success teams also might own or contribute to an online knowledge base that customers can refer to when they are in need of help.

The DCXE is very interested in paths to the knowledge base. Why are customers turning to the knowledge base? Looking at customer journeys that lead to the knowledge base and from there perhaps to a "Contact Us" functionality can reveal customer friction points. We will look into this technique later in the next chapter.

If the customer success team has large contact center operations, there will be even more data the DCXE can utilize to proactively observe and prevent customer friction issues. Call volume metrics around contact queues and contact reasons are good sources of insight. Spikes in call volume for certain queues and reasons are often a sign that analysis is warranted. DCXEs with their customer observability techniques and tools are ideal partners for anyone managing contact centers as their dashboards might provide deeper insights into why certain call spikes occur.

In summary, customer success teams and contact center operations provide ample data and insights to the DCXE, who then focuses on working with the engineering teams in reducing the customer pain points that are technical in nature.

Voice of the Customer (VoC) Program

If your organization has a Voice of the Customer program, the DCXE needs to be associated with it as a representative member of the engineering team.

The VoC program captures valuable information about customers' preferences, experiences, expectations, and aversions. The insights generated from such a program allow the DCXE to search for root causes of possible bottlenecks and pain points in the technology layers of the product or experience. Such active participation by the DCXE brings the engineering team closer to the VoC discussions and helps shorten the feedback loop in case negative customer feedback needs to be worked on by the engineering team.

Another important input to the VoC program is the assistance with the impact analysis of certain reported customer friction points. If one customer raises awareness about a friction point, the DCXE can typically provide insight into which other customers or segments of customers might be impacted. Such a wider search of impact can surface the bigger picture across customer segments.

Sales and Marketing

Sales is typically focused on selling and promoting the digital services of your organization, while marketing works on promoting, selling, and distributing them. In a way, there is some overlap. What's very important for both departments, however, is the engagement and experience customers are having with the products they are selling and advertising.

While both departments have their own ways to determine key data around engagement, conversion, and retention, it is still a good idea for the DCXE to reach out to these departments and work with them to share metrics like engagement and friction trends.

The DCXE might be able to provide a higher level of granularity of insight in some cases, while the sales and marketing department can provide their unique view of the world and let the DCXE calibrate their model of analysis based on inputs from sales and marketing. For example, wouldn't it be beneficial if the DCXE alerts sales about clients experiencing a high degree of friction? This is quite helpful when it comes to renewals, and sales can understand why a customer might not be inclined to renew the service they are selling. A comprehensive analysis prior to the call can lead to discoveries of value to the client, data around the experience issue showing the temporary nature or the road map toward improvement, as well as engagement metrics that show underutilized opportunities. Reviewing the underutilized opportunities can then lead to cross-sell or upsell opportunities during the conversation.

Enabling sales and marketing to do a better job by providing key digital customer experience insights is exceedingly possible and easy. Let's say your organization is collecting customer engagement metrics in Pendo, Heap Analytics, or Google Analytics. The metrics captured there, especially the engagement metrics, should be propagated into the customer relationship software (e.g., Salesforce) and the sales enablement software (e.g., Gainsight). This is quite easy with the effort of a one-time setup via the connectors available for the tools.

A collaboration between sales and marketing leaders and the DCXE could lead to the setup of early alerts preventing churn or the scheduling of conversations about increase in engagement with key features. It could also include the measure of adoption of the features across the client portfolio and the depth within the organization or user base. Marketing would like to receive such metrics to better understand which features should be highlighted during the next campaign to increase engagement, adoption, and utilization, thus increasing the business benefit to the customers.

When the sales department contacted me about the opportunities outlined earlier, we set up a map of all the tools that contain the metrics needed for a successful feed into Salesforce and Gainsight, in our case. Identifying this need in sales strengthened our customer experience observability efforts in engineering and in the product organization. We became partners! We charted the work necessary toward building the customer experience information pipeline and enabling increased sales success powered by customer experience insights.

How-to Guide
Essential techniques

In the previous chapters, we learned about the discipline of digital customer experience engineering, how it is defined, and how the function interacts within an organization dedicated to superior digital customer experience.

This chapter will illustrate the activities and techniques employed by the engineer dedicated to digital customer experience engineering, monitoring, and analytics. The goal of the chapter is to introduce the key concepts available to the DCXE on the path to detecting unnecessary digital customer experience friction.

Typical Activities and Responsibilities

As identified in Chapter 3, the digital customer experience engineer (DCXE) has the goal of crafting and establishing experience observability into customer interactions with the digital product.

The most critical function of the DCXE is to implement observability of digital customer experience pain points, which means establishing a straight line from customer surveys (like NPS) and support escalations to software engineering–related friction. The DCXE utilizes observability techniques iteratively to create the right level of visibility at various stages of the customer journey path or paths.

© Lars Wiedenhoefer 2021
L. Wiedenhoefer, *Digital Customer Experience Engineering*,
https://doi.org/10.1007/978-1-4842-7243-5_6

To maintain observability of issues just in time and without too much delay, it is important to establish a mapping mechanism of customer-reported issues not only to customer success and support teams but also to engineering teams. The DCXE helps in creating this mapping. For such a mapping, the DCXE would establish traceability between survey tools, the support CRM, and the engineering observability tools. Once this is created, it becomes easier for the software engineering teams to directly empathize with customer feedback, because it's traceable and observable, and easier to do something about it – quicker than ever before, thus shortening the feedback cycle drastically.

Other typical activities and responsibilities may include the following.

Customer Experience Observability Program Governance

Establishing the positive acceleration cycle as identified in Figure 3-2 might require the establishment of a special strategic program inside the engineering organization that's focused on creating the right level of customer experience observability. The DCXE assists in setting up the program's mission and goals, measuring and reporting program success and milestones, reporting the value created by the program, and going through strict scope management.

For a program goal, you might consider lowering the bar to entry to gaining customer experience insights. You might say the stated goal is to increase customer-facing engineering teams' ability to gain actionable insights while decreasing customer experience friction. The former could be measured by the rate the engineering team discovers actionable insights and removes customer friction items and conversion or engagement bottlenecks. The latter can be measured by a reduction in the rate of customer service escalations to the engineering team for specific topics of focus.

Be aware that such a program doesn't come to existence just by itself. There needs to be an awareness in the organization that such an investment has business benefits. Also note that the DCXE needs an executive sponsor to enable the program to succeed.

Cross-Team Alignment and Communication

As identified in Chapter 5, the DCXE is involved in connecting a variety of cross-functional teams to the effort of increasing customer experience observability. The DCXE should not underestimate the effort behind making and maintaining the connections and strategically plan this portion of the work as it is necessary and essential to the acceleration function of the DCXE role.

A focus should be given on enabling the communication through technical enablers and accelerators. The idea here is to enable the communication via data that lead to insights and, subsequently, conversations, alignment, and positive actions improving the customer experience. The DCXE needs to enable connections between tools. For example, when the customer journey analytics tool is linked to the session replay tool, the product owner can quickly go from high-level flow analysis to friction detection. That's an example of empowering the product owner. Another example is to empower the sales leader by linking the sales tools to the customer experience analytics tool. This will allow the sales leader to see data around the feature usage and utilization, which has the power to guide sales conversation at renewal time or helps with cross-sell or upsell opportunities, to name a few use cases.

The point is for the DCXE to maintain communication with external roles in order to evangelize the benefits of customer experience insights and to collect concrete requirements from other functions for implementations that lead to the betterment of the digital customer experience.

Customer Experience Observability and Traceability Tools

As with any engineering craft, increasing customer experience observability comes along with a strategic interplay of tools. Leading the evaluation of tools that present the right fit for the organization is a key role for the DCXE.

The tools range from simple spreadsheets to observability tools mapping the customer journey, to tools providing experience replays and friction detection, to tools providing insights into the engineering site quality and performance in relation to the customer experience. There are even tools that accelerate the sentiment interpretation of customer escalation and survey feedback at scale.

Identifying which tool fits the organization best during their customer experience improvement journey is rewarding and can even go along with cost savings. Cost savings come from the orchestration and alignment of the essential tools to get to insights the quickest and from decommissioning tools that are not needed anymore. For example, how many journey mapping tools do you need? If you find that your organization utilizes several, there's an opportunity for cost savings and alignment.

Customer-Focused Input into the CI/CD Pipeline

There are several areas where DCXE-provided insights are valuable to the technical team's CI/CD (Continuous Integration/Continuous Delivery) pipeline.

Test coverage, may it be unit test coverage, functional, or end-to-end coverage, is an area where the DCXE can provide customer usage insights to guide test planning. The DCXE can answer critical coverage questions regarding feature and customer path coverage.

Input, for example, can be gathered via adoption and engagement metrics. Test coverage should be concentrated in the feature areas that are critical and most utilized. A feature adoption analysis as in Figure 6-1 could reveal that 4% of features drive 80% of the customer engagement measured in feature clicks. Such a graph is easily derived from Pendo.io, a very useful customer experience analytics tool.

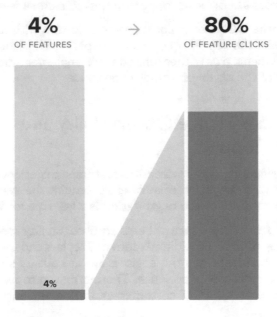

Figure 6-1. Feature adoption analysis in Pendo

Given that 4% of features are critical to 80% of the customer interactions, the DCXE would advise the testing engineers to focus on these features first when designing a regression test suite.

Providing the engineers with insights into the customer behavior, for example, via journey paths, would further provide insights into how to model the tests as they should cover the customer journey paths well. Both Pendo.io and Heap.io, for example, provide excellent resources for capturing journey paths. Moving along journey paths allows the test engineers to create test cases that exactly follow customer behaviors.

For new features, the interaction works differently. The test engineer builds hypotheses of how the customer would use the feature and builds out the test cases based on these hypotheses. After production release, the DCXE would then provide insights into the feature adoption and journey path and guide the test engineer in validating if the hypotheses were actually true. If they turn out to be wrong, the DCXE can provide the insights and data necessary to build better test cases for reuse as regression cases.

Enabling Speeding Up the Analysis of Customer Feedback and Sentiment

Many organizations keep the customer feedback in support tickets, customer reviews, or NPS survey feedback inaccessible to the engineering team. This is normally a very smart move as nobody wants to flood the engineering team with too much information.

I've been in situations where reading through the entire issue documentation about an installation project took two weeks to analyze. I did take the needed time to extract the insights needed for my engineering team. While this yielded important information, the method was just not scalable. Luckily, I discussed this scenario with the machine learning and data science team. A few weeks later, they produced a tool utilizing Python NLP (natural language processing) that cut down on the analysis from two weeks to five minutes! Yes, within five minutes anyone who wanted to know could see the engineering hot buttons of any of the projects going on.

The DCXE should work with their engineering team to enable such analysis. Focused information about customer hot buttons enables engineering teams to provide input during ongoing planning with their product owner. Necessary information about impact and urgency on a specific feedback item can be gleaned from such a tool.

The DCXE could even install such analytics if they have access to AWS. Amazon created AWS Comprehend, which provides a tutorial on the topic "Analyzing Insights from Customer Reviews." The tutorial takes only one hour to complete after setting up the prerequisites! Gaining access to valuable customer sentiment within one hour is time well spent. My recommendation is to export the support queue and NPS information for use with the tutorial to make the effort more applicable. Once the value is proven, it might make sense to automate the extraction of support queue and NPS information on a regular basis.

The section "Speed Up the Analysis of Customer Feedback Received via the Support Channel" reviews further details and other options for speeding up the collection of deeper insights into the customer feedback streams, be it NPS comments, support cases, or other feedback items.

Increasing the Signal-to-Noise Ratio of Alerting Tools

Tools like PagerDuty or Sentry can be invaluable when it comes to receiving alerts for production issues and errors. Unfortunately, when they are not configured correctly, they can become the proverbial situation where they "cry wolf" too often and get ignored. Engineers are in a tough spot if they ignore such a tool one wrong time as any of these alerts could be harbingers of a production mayhem or escalation. They are also in a tough spot if they attend to noisy alerts that lead to nothing. They wear out, don't trust these tools, and can't focus on their regular work.

How can the DCXE help in this situation? The DCXE does not own setting up PagerDuty or Sentry or any other alerting tool. The teams do. The DCXE should, however, be a master of the observability tools that can provide critical insight into the customer impact of error alerts and can thus help with tuning the tools. Over time, more meaningful alerts will occur, and engineers get acquainted with the observability tools to assess impact. And the next time a PagerDuty alert triggers that is not related to any measurable impact, the alert can be put on the list of candidates for deletion from PagerDuty for noise reduction.

Outside of tools like PagerDuty or Sentry, the DCXE collaborates with the SRE team on setting up and understanding the monitors for the four golden signals – latency, errors, saturation, traffic (per Google's SRE book).

When it comes to "latency," the DCXE is interested in the response time of successful service requests triggered by digital customer interactions.

For example, how long did it take to render a user interface page or how long did it take for a form submission to be acknowledged? Per Google's SRE book, it is important for the DCXE to collaborate with SRE in their focus on the "latency of failed requests." How are these handled and how are they impacting the customer experience? For example, are 500 errors (server-side errors) handled well? Ideally, a 500 error doesn't impact the customer because there might be redundancy implemented, and the server having issues might gracefully fail over. There are, of course, times when this doesn't happen, and such errors have customer impact as the service request triggered by the customer won't be fulfilled. In the latency category of the four golden signals, the DCXE is interested in asking the SRE team to work with engineering on ensuring the errors are detected expediently and handled well. Fast error detection is naturally better than slow error detection! It's such an obvious thing to say, but having seen important errors languish because there was just too much noise makes me call for quickly detecting the errors that matter most.

"Errors" in the four golden signals focus on the "rate of requests that fail," per Google's SRE book. The DCXE works on the detection of scenarios where errors impact the customer and works with DevOps and SRE to reduce the error frequency and the impact of the error. Is the error, when unavoidable, clearly described to the customer? Can they recover from it by perhaps trying the request again? Is there assistance offered when an error occurs via a knowledge article or a clear link to the company's support page? The DCXE also works on measuring the impact of the errors on the customer. The DCXE works to identify which errors are impactful and need to be mitigated. The section "Calibrate Alerts – From Noise to Important Customer Impact Signals" goes into how this can be accomplished.

"Saturation" of a service measures how packed a service is. For example, is the database going to be full soon? If it fills up, subsequent requests will be ignored, which has customer impact. This is an example of how SRE and DCXE need to collaborate to proactively mitigate potential customer experience impact.

On the "traffic" side of the four golden signals, the DCXE is interested in seeing monitoring and alerting is in place measuring the demand rate of the system. A customer experience example that might be relatable to many readers is releases of popular game consoles for which oftentimes the ecommerce systems trying to sell the most popular ones are not calibrated to handle the increase in demand. This doesn't only lead to customer frustration but missed revenue opportunities.

Support Engineering Escalation Analysis

Impact analysis as described earlier is not only important for engineers receiving a PagerDuty alert. It is equally important to support engineers receiving escalations from customers. It is very critical for them to identify the impact quickly in order to determine the priority or criticality of the issue.

The DCXE can assist here in providing guidance in the use of the observability tools.

In the article "Use Dev Tools to See the Impact of Performance on Conversions," Hanna Woodward describes how to measure the impact poor site performance has on a digital experience using FullStory and explains why this is needed:

> Website performance influences revenue through things like conversion rates, shopping cart size or abandonment, customer loyalty, brand awareness, and other KPIs. At a high level, this is why Chief Revenue Officers care about performance. They want to know if something is broken and preventing customers from checking out, or if slow speeds are throwing a wrench in their revenue targets.

The DCXE can create an impact funnel constructed in FullStory relevant to escalated errors or degraded performance, like slow page loads. Clues of what to include in the funnel analysis can be found in the escalation ticket. If the escalation ticket is not very conclusive, the DCXE could take the impact time of the error and subsequently search for the session to observe the escalated error. With the gained information, the DCXE could then be able to craft a funnel that includes all customers entering a certain experience and then subsequently experiencing the issue.

Hanna Woodward used the technique of contrasting funnels to compare the impact of the issue with the issue funnel against the funnel containing customers not experiencing the issue.

Again, such information is invaluable in determining the criticality and urgency of a customer support situation.

Identify and Map to Key User Journeys and Touchpoints

In her article "Getting to grips with Customer Experience Observability," Sorcha McNamee explains in detail how to map out key customer journey paths in Heap Analytics. From there, she builds conversion funnels to measure conversions, and, using the reverse funnel, she analyzes conversion friction points.

> *Mapping out how you expect customers to use your application is a really useful place to start! Mapping out your customer journey allows you to visualise the full journey a customer will go on and then observe them accordingly. Once your customer journeys have been outlined the next part is selecting the key touch points in where you want to observe and gain feedback.*
>
> —Sorcha McNamee, "Getting to grips with Customer Experience Observability"

Heap Analytics describes the technique of creating and analyzing funnels on their Help Center site named *Funnel*. The tool makes it relatively easy to create meaningful experience funnels as illustrated in Figure 6-2.

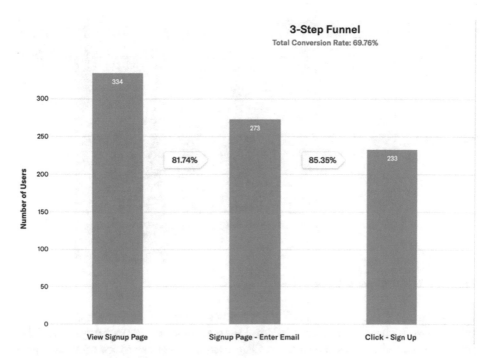

Figure 6-2. Three-step funnel in Heap Analytics

When a DCXE sees a conversion rate of 69.76%, they immediately wonder if the drop of 30.24% is related to customer experience friction–related issues. They will build the reverse funnel focusing on the 30.24% to investigate the individual sessions deeper. They may use journey paths to identify what happened to customers that didn't successfully complete their journey as expected.

Looking at journey paths is also an investigative technique Sorcha McNamee describes and actively uses to identify how customers successfully or unsuccessfully completed their journey.

Her advice is clear:

> *It helps you target a certain event and better understand why conversion rate isn't as high as you would expect.*
>
> —Sorcha McNamee, "Getting to grips with Customer Experience Observability"

Heap Analytics describes the technique of creating paths and path reports on their Help Center site named *Paths*. The tool makes it relatively easy to create path views as illustrated in Figure 6-3.

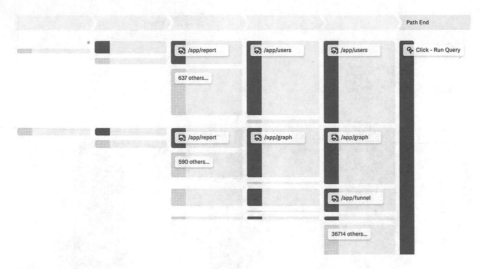

Figure 6-3. Customer paths using Heap Analytics

Using this technique, the DCXE will quickly see where customers came from, which events they interacted with, and where they ended up. Sometimes, the paths are straightforward and clear. Other times, they are more confusing and require more investigation. And more investigation of areas where the customer behavior is not clear leads to valuable usability insights and ultimately increases conversions or even new features or products if the insights are acted upon.

Armed with the insights from the aforementioned techniques, the DCXE drives positive change on behalf of the customer. In fact, Sorcha McNamee reminds the reader:

> After gathering insights it doesn't just stop there, what we do with this information is one of the most important parts of the customer observability process. We need to inform Product and UX of our findings. Create a ticket with all the relevant information and have a conversation with the Product Manager/Owner & UX to let them know the findings. Getting as many members from different disciplines involved in this process is critical.

—Sorcha McNamee, "Getting to grips with Customer Experience Observability"

Having identified conversion or success funnels and journey paths in a tool like Heap Analytics yields the sessions that need to be investigated further when friction or potential for friction got detected. A closer look is sometimes needed to relate to what the customer exactly experienced. For such a closer look, a session playback tool is needed. Session playback tools, such as FullStory, are able to play back the sessions in the same way the customer experienced them.

You may have established traceability between tools like Heap and FullStory by either linking sessions directly or sharing ids (user id, customer id, correlation id, etc.). It is important to establish some kind of linking as you want to be able to identify trends in one tool and observe them in the other tool as well.

For further reading regarding correlation ids, I recommend Annette McCullough's blog *Correlating Log Messages* where she says

> *When working in a distributed architecture, particularly one that utilises asynchronous patterns, it can become increasingly difficult to gain an understanding of the journey that messages take through the system and how they conclude. One approach to mitigating this pain point, is the use of a Correlation Identifier.*

So, in this case, you identified a funnel drop in Heap and noticed sessions you want to look up in FullStory. If you have an id that describes the same event in both places, such as a correlation id, you can copy it from Heap into the search in FullStory and watch the event.

I am using the example of FullStory as they are describing the creation and use of funnels well on their help page article "Can I create and visualize funnels?". They created a funnel for users that added something to a cart, went to the checkout page, and clicked checkout (see Figure 6-4).

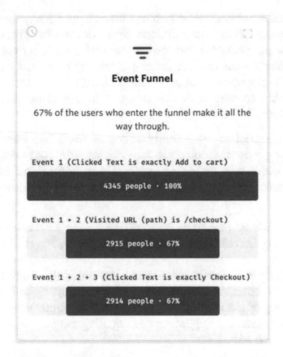

Figure 6-4. Checkout funnel using FullStory

As it is clear from the funnel, 67% of customers are successful in the checkout experience. For a digital customer experience engineer, it is critical to look deeper into the 33% that were not successful. What exactly happened to these sessions? Where quantities not available? Where payments not successful? Or did perhaps system errors prevent the checkout? Questions like these can easily yield answers by looking at the affected sessions.

In order to surface the affected sessions, a reverse funnel needs to get constructed. In FullStory, this is quite simple as Figure 6-5 illustrates.

EVENT FILTERS · Find people who performed these events   in this order   and   across any number of sessions

| 1 | Clicked ∨ | Text is exactly ∨ | Add to cart | or ⋯ | ⬤ ⧉ + ✕ |
| 2 | Visited URL ∨ | is ∨ | PATH ∨ /checkout | or ⋯ | ⬤ |

Exclude people who performed these events

| Clicked ∨ | Text is exactly ∨ | Checkout | or ⋯ | ⬤ ⧉ + ✕ |

Figure 6-5. Constructing a reverse funnel in FullStory

The event filters 1 and 2 stay untouched. Only the third query in the original funnel needs to get reversed. In FullStory, it is as simple as asking the tool to exclude the sessions with the successful checkout experience. So, a reverse funnel is nothing but the technique of visualizing the customer sessions that did not confirm to the desired funnel experience for one reason or the other. Analyzing the sessions this query yields will then provide the needed insights that are needed to enhance the checkout experience.

The results of this process are evident: customer experience issues are observable and ready to get socialized quicker. Providing the engineering department with such a level of observability adds to active voices in the discussion of issues with the support, product, and UX teams. Additional voices are key in identifying issues earlier and proactively while accelerating the process of fixing issues and gaining the necessary buy-ins for what exactly to fix.

Why Are Customers Seeking Help?

A special case of analyzing customer paths as described in the previous section is the investigation of customers contacting the help function of your business.

Customers clicking through to the FAQ section or even the Contact Us section indicate they are in need of special help. They might have a case at hand not considered in the design of the product or feature. Or they might need to report that the feature doesn't work well anymore. Regardless of why they are reaching out via these sections, they need help, and taking a look at such sessions can be of valuable insights to the DCXE.

Recently, I have had to click through to Contact Us for AT&T as the statement section wasn't available anymore. I had no way of seeing the statement when I clicked the button that should have gotten me to the statement section. On the mobile experience, I was directed to the upgrades section. On the desktop experience, I was presented with a page only showing my account number and the regular AT&T footer page. Note, this story is not a dig at AT&T as I am very happy with their services. It is just raising awareness that customer experience friction can happen to all of us.

Now, think about how many people called AT&T that day. Let's say their cost per call is $10 and 1000 customers called. That's $10,000 spent on an experience issue on a single day. Of course, the real numbers are different, but this is to illustrate how quickly costs of customer experience issues can impact the revenue of a company.

At PayPal, I used to have exact numbers of cost per call and impact counts of customer experience issues related to contact center volume increases. A DCXE armed with such information can easily make the business case of having call center volume impacting customer experience issues removed.

This is a strong encouragement to start by measuring how many customers reach out to your company's Contact Us page. Follow and analyze the impacted sessions and start calculating the impact to your business.

Establish Customer Engagement Tracking

New features get released frequently while existing users rely on certain features they learned to love. The introduction of new features could either delight customers or confuse them. Or, in some cases, existing customers might not have discovered existing features. Such a lack of feature engagement might result in reduced renewal rates or revenue. Stemming off lack of engagement is not only the job of the product and client services teams. Of course, they should stay on top of customer engagement. Engineers, frequently releasing new features, should be interested to measure the feature adoption as well. If there is anything of technical nature preventing engagement, they should be aware of the situation. The DCXE needs to set up engagement dashboards to stay on top of engagement metrics.

With Figure 6-1 in this chapter, it became apparent how Pendo.io is helping with the feature adoption analysis.

Heap Analytics discusses the topic of feature adoption in their article "How to improve customer health with Heap's new Account Health Analysis feature." In their article, they walk through the setup of how to measure the adoption of a feature by a customer account. In their example, they discuss the adoption of the "Intercom Integration" as an example feature.

Figure 6-6 shows how easy the setup is.

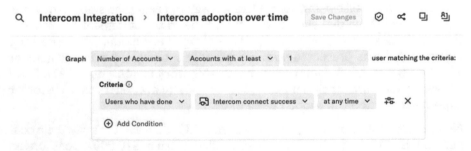

Figure 6-6. Feature adoption in Heap Analytics

Simply count the "users who have done" the action of "Intercom connect success." Note that the "Intercom connect success" action is something that needs to be mapped within Heap Analytics. Such an action is easy to set up and map.

Tracking adoption over time might yield a graph like in Figure 6-7. Knowing that the feature adoption raises over time is quite satisfying, and there might have been certain events associated with the sudden raise in the graph. Now, imagine if the adoption doesn't increase in the way it was predicted! Look at the sessions where the customer did adopt the new feature. Have a look to see if there are any friction elements. Are customers seeing errors that they have to struggle through? Are they just getting lost before they finally find the feature?

Intercom adoption over time

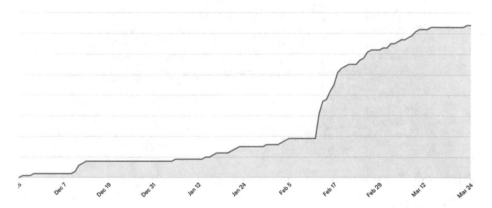

Figure 6-7. Feature adoption over time

To further study the art of capturing user adoption, it is recommended to read Tomer Sharon's work "Measuring user adoption" on Medium. Tomer Sharon's user adoption model in Figure 6-8 shows the quadrants that need to be taken in consideration when studying user adoption. KEI in the figure stands for "Key Experience Indicator."

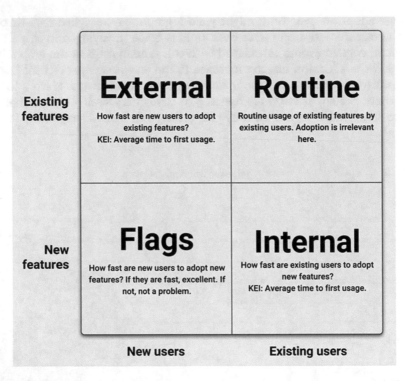

Figure 6-8. Tomer Sharon's user adoption model

For the DCXE, this model is very useful as they need to put measures in place using Heap Analytics or other tools. This is especially important when customer feature adoption is measured with new releases. First of all, set up measures that fall in the *Routine* quadrant. Any major drop of usage could indicate interference of a new feature with existing routine usage. It might be desired if the new feature replaces routine usage of existing features. But if that's not the case, measures of routine usage need to be put in place as a safeguard measurement that could, for example, catch regression bugs.

Graphs for *Internal*, *Flags*, and *External* are very helpful when an engineering team wants to measure how their new feature release fares over time. The team should discuss the release results with the product owner. The DCXE should contribute session insights that validate the feature success or exemplify friction items necessitating improvements or even a release rollback.

Establish Customer Retention Tracking

Measuring customer retention is key for your business as acquiring new customers is many times more expensive than retaining existing customers. For the engineering team, it is insightful to see customer retention in regard to certain experiences and features. If a certain feature is supposed to contribute to retention, it might be good to establish a measure to see if this project goal was realized.

> *To ensure customers keep returning to your site, the most fundamental thing that you need is a quality product/service. There's simply no getting around this if you are in the business for the long haul.*

> —Tracy Vides, "Reimagining Your Website
> As A Tool For Customer Retention"

To the DCXE, this means retention needs to be visualized in order to investigate digital experiences of customers where retention is achieved or is not achieved.

Establishing a retention graph for further analysis is quite easy. Heap.io describes this on their *Retention* help section.

Two events are needed: the start event and the return event. For the start event, record the first interaction the customer might have with your service or site. Typically, this is the new account creation. The return event is the interaction you want to track that most customers are doing when they come back. It might even be the event that is most important to your business or of interest in your investigation. For example, in a financial services environment, you might care about how many people log in to their account and check their balance. Or, because you just activated the feature, you want to know how many returning customers are making payments via Zelle. So, in this example, the start event is the user registration for the financial service establishing the account and the eligibility of making Zelle payments. The return event to be tracked here is the navigation of logged-in customers to the Zelle service page. Please note that you don't necessarily want to measure, in this context, how many customers successfully submitted a Zelle payment. For this, the funnel analysis is a better fit.

The resulting graph of a retention analysis in Heap Analytics would look like the graph in Figure 6-9.

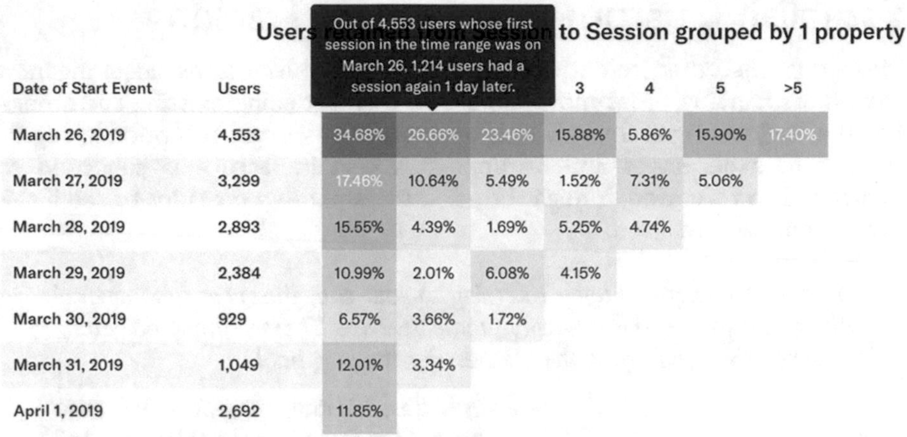

Users re[...] to Session grouped by 1 property

> Out of 4,553 users whose first session in the time range was on March 26, 1,214 users had a session again 1 day later.

Date of Start Event	Users				3	4	5	>5
March 26, 2019	4,553	34.68%	26.66%	23.46%	15.88%	5.86%	15.90%	17.40%
March 27, 2019	3,299	17.46%	10.64%	5.49%	1.52%	7.31%	5.06%	
March 28, 2019	2,893	15.55%	4.39%	1.69%	5.25%	4.74%		
March 29, 2019	2,384	10.99%	2.01%	6.08%	4.15%			
March 30, 2019	929	6.57%	3.66%	1.72%				
March 31, 2019	1,049	12.01%	3.34%					
April 1, 2019	2,692	11.85%						

Figure 6-9. Retention analysis with Heap Analytics

This graph shows that the five-day retention of customers visiting the site on March 26 was 17.40%. If your business would expect a higher retention figure, it might be a good idea to study samples of the users who did not return. Did they perhaps have negative experiences in the form of errors? Are items added to shopping carts not available? Or does the checkout process take too long? Perhaps the customers were looking for incentives, didn't find any, and gave up. Whatever the reason may be, a strategic analysis of retention is quite helpful to uncover how to provide experiences that make customers come back.

Google Analytics makes retention analytics quite easy as well. Figure 6-10 shows a comparative analysis of all users against direct traffic to a site, which happens to be the site of my family's vacation rental property. Google Analytics makes it quite easy to compare cohorts of all users during weekly time intervals against cohorts of users in the Direct Traffic segment. Direct Traffic, in this case, means that the users knew how to find the property directly vs. finding us via Instagram, for example.

Week 0	Week 1	Week 2	Week 3	Week 4	Week 5	Week 6
100.00%	5.56%	0.00%	0.00%	0.00%	0.00%	0.00%
100.00%	8.70%	0.00%	0.00%	0.00%	0.00%	0.00%
100.00%	0.00%	0.00%	0.00%	0.00%	0.00%	
100.00%	0.00%	0.00%	0.00%	0.00%		
100.00%	14.29%	0.00%	0.00%			
100.00%	0.00%	0.00%				
100.00%	0.00%					
100.00%	4.44%	0.00%	0.00%	0.00%	0.00%	0.00%
100.00%	5.88%	0.00%	0.00%	0.00%	0.00%	0.00%
100.00%	0.00%	0.00%	0.00%	0.00%	0.00%	
100.00%	0.00%	0.00%	0.00%	0.00%		
100.00%	25.00%	0.00%	0.00%			
100.00%	0.00%	0.00%				
100.00%	0.00%					

Figure 6-10. Retention analysis with Google Analytics

It is quite interesting to see that there was a high week 1 retention for Direct Traffic during a week where 25% of the users came back. For this particular week, it is worthwhile to study the cohort of customers further. Insights from such a discovery might drive toward long-term retention and customers coming back more frequently.

To get started with Google Analytics' Cohort Analysis (this is how the retention analytics feature is called), I recommend Patrick Han's article "A Beginner's Guide to Cohort Analysis: the Most Actionable (and Underrated) Report on Google Analytics" on Medium.

> A "cohort analysis," then, simply allows you to compare the behavior and metrics of different cohorts over time. You can then find the highest-performing (or lowest-performing) cohorts, and what factors are driving this performance.
>
> —Patrick Han, "A Beginner's Guide to Cohort Analysis: the Most Actionable (and Underrated) Report on Google Analytics"

How does digital customer experience engineering fit in? This is a valid question, as cohort or retention analysis is typically done by other departments outside of engineering. The DCXE helps here by making sample sessions of the relevant customer cohorts available, which leads to further insights and great conversations with the product owner, but also drives toward ruling out that customer friction items based on engineering are the root cause of the retention loss.

Create a Digital Representation of Customer Journey Success

How do you express the quality of the digital experiences provided by your product or platform?

A quantitative way to answer this question is to pull together the prior three chapters regarding funnels, engagement, and retention: If the sum of all funnels behaves well compared to the baselined and expected funnel drops, the users are adequately engaging with the features, and coming back at a rate that is satisfactory and positive to the business you are in, you could say you have built a quantitative way to measure a baselined state of quality. This model can be used to improve upon from the baseline, to alert when the quantitative quality and performance of the model degrades, and to study sessions for insights into improvement opportunities.

To set this up, look at the sum of experiences or journey paths. First, these paths need to be captured and understood. Start with the business-critical paths, identify the intermediate steps at the right level, and define their individual start point and end point.

Once all relevant journey paths are defined, map them out in a pictorial view similar to Figure 6-11.

Figure 6-11. Example end-to-end customer journey

The next step is to define all interaction funnels that characterize the end-to-end experience(s) well. Build a dashboard of funnel analytics lining up the funnels (representing the customer journeys) consecutively or hierarchically to form a likeness of the customer experience. Baseline the funnel performance and set alarms if the baseline performance deviates from the actual performance.

For example, start out with the end-to-end funnel as pictured in Figure 6-12.

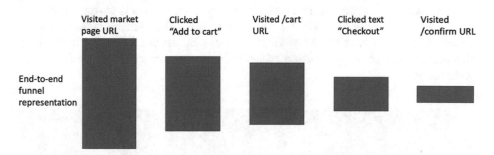

Figure 6-12. End-to-end funnel example

Follow the performance of this funnel in production and have a discussion with your product owner in order to baseline its performance. Once a baseline is established, set alerts in case the funnel's performance drops outside of a desired range. Also note that you might need to baseline funnels for seasonal performance. For example, you would expect a higher conversion rate during high traffic shopping season, and a serious funnel drop would cause much damage and warrants an alert and immediate investigation.

To set funnel alerts, measure the customers who went to checkout and successfully purchased something (in the example, this means they would visit the /confirm URL). Set a fixed alert to alert if checkouts drop below a certain value (i.e., the baseline) or they drop below a level compared to last week's or last month's numbers.

In Figure 6-13, the alert triggers when the number of customers who went to checkout and successfully purchased something drops below 45.

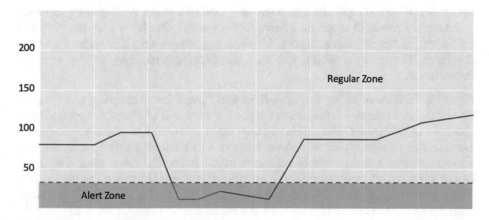

Figure 6-13. Funnel traffic alert example

You also want to set an alert looking after customer experience errors. In this example, track any errors experienced during the shopping and purchasing experiences. Let's say your site's error rate in the end-to-end shopping experience is below 50 errors a day on any given day. In this case, you want to be alerted if errors raise significantly above 50 errors a day. In Figure 6-14, the alert is set to trigger when the number of errors rises above 55 at any given time.

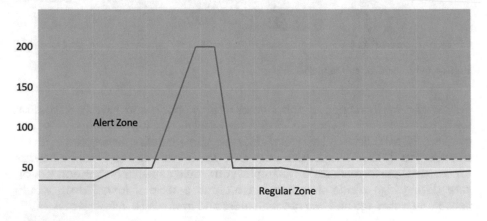

Figure 6-14. Error rate alert example

For a step-by-step guide to setting up alerts in FullStory, for example, turn to their *Introduction to Alerts* page.

After setting up the funnel measures and alerts for the end-to-end flow, the next step is to identify the detailed experiences that need closer monitoring via funnel analysis and alerts.

In the shopping example, an area to highlight would be the checkout experience as there are multiple steps determining the overall checkout success. Multiple paths might be of interest here, illuminating funnel drops for the payment methods, the address entry, the various shipping methods, or the coupon experience.

Figure 6-15 illustrates an example flow and funnel for measuring the coupon to checkout success. In this example, the first drop of all shoppers who visited the cart vs. shoppers who applied coupons is expected as not everybody has coupons to present. The next drop warrants more investigation, as not many shoppers who tried to apply coupons made it to the next step. The root cause needs to be investigated. Which kind of errors are preventing customers from proceeding? The DCXE will look at sessions to identify if technical friction elements are at the core of the rapid funnel drop issue.

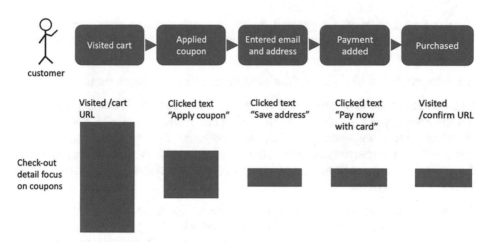

Figure 6-15. Coupon funnel example

The technical team should collaborate with their product team and identify how many detailed flows are captured via detailed funnel flows.

In partnership with the quality engineer, the DCXE ensures the identified funnels are represented as regression tests pre-release. This will ensure the team tests that the product was built right. The DCXE sets up monitoring and alerting around the funnels via observability tools in order to ensure the team built the right product for the customer, a product without technical friction.

Quality is therefore established by testing the product well pre-release, using the discovered paths customers mostly take as a baseline for regression tests. Post-release, the DCXE seeks optimal technical performance of the customer experience by investigating and observing the journey flows and funnel baselines.

Detect and Remove Customer Friction

Before identifying customer friction, let's determine how to define it. Sean Johnson defined customer friction as

Anything in your product that represents a barrier to adoption or growth.

—Sean Johnson, "How to Minimize Product Friction"

If it can be "anything," it is of course hard to look for. Thus, it is paramount to identify patterns of friction that guide the investigation toward the reduction of friction elements. And by removing digital technical friction elements, the DCXE, together with the technical teams and product teams, removes the barriers to adoption or growth. It is now self-evident that a continuous endeavor of reducing customer friction becomes the flywheel of success as it enables growth.

So, how does the DCXE methodically detect the customer friction?

We discussed looking into funnel drops and their potential root causes earlier. As discussed, the funnels can be observed and investigated with tools such as Pendo.io, Heap Analytics, or Google Analytics. The sessions marking the drop-offs in completion of tasks, that is, all the sessions that don't reach the funnel end point, mark potential friction points and should be investigated via session replay tools.

Looking at all the sessions in the funnel drop scenarios can be quite time-consuming. This is why modern customer experience observation tools create ways to automatically capture and classify certain indications of friction. Is there a more systematic way to find certain indicators of friction?

For example, FullStory discusses "frustration signals" in their article "The guide to understanding user frustration online." Here, they are identified as

> Including Rage Clicks, Dead Clicks, Error Clicks, Form Abandonment, and Thrashing mouse.
>
> —FullStory, "The guide to understanding user frustration online"

They are illustrated in Figure 6-16.

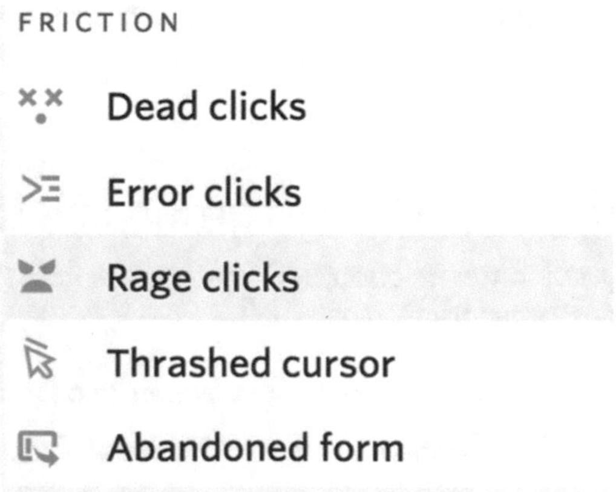

FRICTION

ˣ˟ Dead clicks

>Ξ Error clicks

Rage clicks

Thrashed cursor

Abandoned form

Figure 6-16. Customer friction captured within FullStory

FullStory makes it relatively easy to detect these issues as sessions are bundled into these categories as such "frustration signals" occur.

Rage clicks occur when users repeatedly click at a high frequency on a digital object. For example, the customer might have spent considerable time building a shopping cart and wants to submit payment, but the "Submit" button doesn't seem to work. It is quite understandable that frustration builds up and is channeled through repeatedly clicking the "Submit" button.

Dead clicks are clicks into spaces on a web page that do not have any effect. The customer might be in a flow of action and expects a button to be at a normal space and clicks in this general area where the button used to be. A recent version change might have changed the button's location and caused friction for this customer example. For the DCXE, it is recommended to investigate such scenarios. How many customers are impacted? How many customers are recovering from a moment of consternation? Is there a lasting friction pattern that must be discussed with the product team? For example, if an important button moved and half of the customers are not finding it anymore and thus not progressing successfully through the site's conversion flow, a case needs to be made to either educate the customers better of the new location of the important button or to put it back to the place where they expect it to be in the first place.

When a customer is faced with a site error and has to click to acknowledge the error, this is called an "error click." Bundling error clicks into a bucket for investigation can be quite helpful. Indeed, valid errors like invalid password credential–related issues might fall into such a bucket. More often than not, there is a treasure trove of interesting customer-impacting issues in this bucket. For example, very cryptic issues such as "Unknown error." The DCXE should look into the root cause of the error and the impact it has on the customer experience. Armed with such information, the DCXE needs to advocate for the removal of the identified customer friction.

Who loves to fill out forms? While forms are necessary, filling out forms is something users don't necessarily like. When they just give up – either at the onset or by not completing the form – and subsequently abandon the page, that's called form abandonment.

Observing sessions where customers abandon a form is a rich hunting ground for customer friction insights. In a shopping cart conversion analysis for a national telecommunications provider in the southern hemisphere, I noticed once a form abandonment rate of over 98%. The forms were so onerous that the majority of their online customers in this country would not be able to purchase a phone plan with them. After multiple stages of forms to be filled out, they just gave up. This key insight was an excellent starting point of a conversation around making the collection of information from the customer easier.

Have you ever moved your mouse pointer or cursor around erratically on the screen out of frustration? I certainly do this when I get lost. This behavior is called "mouse thrashing" or "cursor thrashing" and is another indication for potential customer friction. It is typically observed when customers are startled and are trying to orient themselves as to where to go next. It might be an indication of confusing options, too many items in a list or a view of choices the customer didn't expect. Whatever it is, such events, when they occur frequently around a specific area, are worth looking into.

Another way to identify possible user friction is by looking at heatmaps. Hotjar, for example, is a software tool visualizing heatmaps of the customer journey as illustrated in Figure 6-17.

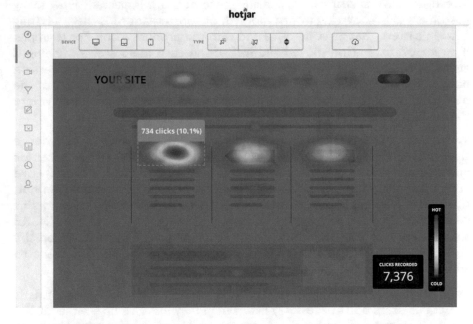

Figure 6-17. Heatmap illustration using Hotjar

The DCXE uses a heatmap visualization tool to observe "dark zones," which are areas a customer was expected to engage in but didn't for some reason. These heatmaps identify if a customer didn't reach a certain area as they just didn't know to scroll to the information they might have needed. Or they simply didn't find a feature because the object, perhaps a button, didn't stand out to them.

Let's also take a look at how LogRocket helps with systematically making issues visible. The Issue Summary page categorizes the issues with the highest severity.

The Issues page enables users to review all their frontend issues in one place and prioritize and learn more about the issues that are actually affecting the customer experience. The histogram at the top provides a quick snapshot of the health of your application by summarizing the number of sessions that are experiencing high-impact issues, low-impact issues, and no issues.

—LogRocket, *Issues*

Figure 6-18 illustrates how this looks on the screen.

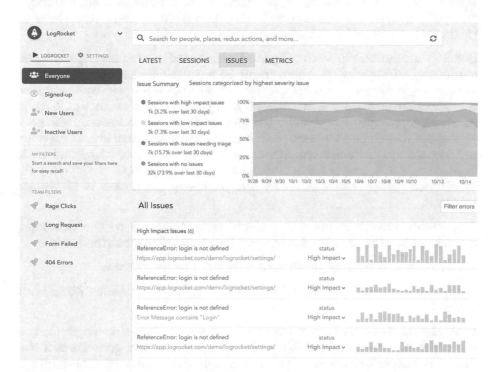

Figure 6-18. LogRocket Issue Summary page

The engineer can quickly arrive at an idea of the issue severity and issue distribution and then click the relevant sessions impacted by the issues.

Calibrate Alerts – From Noise to Important Customer Impact Signals

When it comes to alerts, there is plenty of opportunity to be suddenly bombarded with noise. I've conducted an alerting analysis and noticed that one software development engineer received 4000+ alerts per month while performing on-call duty. That's 129 per day! Of course, this is an extreme case, but a reminder that the alerting situation needs to be taken seriously, and a structured approach is needed to avoid such paralyzing extremes.

Sentry.io might directly stream error notifications to your team's slack channel, and PagerDuty might alert you of issues regarding some 500 error limit overrun that was just triggered. It's all very convenient, but such "convenient" alerts get out of hand fast.

Even teams that have their alerts organized according to the "four golden signals" principle of monitoring per Google's SRE book, namely, "latency," "traffic," "errors," and "saturation," still are in need to assess the alerts in relation to customer impact when such alerts are triggered.

Building a relationship with triggered alerts and customer impact helps immensely during triaging. There might be a situation where multiple alerts are coming in. Or an alert is competing with another work priority. Whatever the situation might be, it is necessary, in the moment when the alert is received, to quickly understand if the alert needs to be addressed right now or if it can wait to be addressed later. If the underlying system imbalance does not impact the customer experience at all, why drop everything and fix it immediately? Of course, if it's understood that the 500 error example mentioned earlier indicates a site outage, immediate action is of course required.

The desire now is to make the alerts easily traceable to the customer experience in order to have a customer impact assessment at the ready.

Let's review two ways by which such linking can be established.

One way is to configure your important customer experience flows with alerts.

Let's say you have built your customer experience funnel in LogRocket, a customer experience observability tool. You want to configure alerts if the funnel is nonperformant or if there is a high error concentration above a threshold. LogRocket allows you to configure such alerts and to send them to PagerDuty to make the on-call engineer aware of the situation.

The benefit of this approach is the immediate link between alert and impact to the customer experience volume. The customer experience funnel or experience path is a representation of the current customer interaction. If it is impacted in any way and the impact triggers an alert, the impact can be directly and quantitatively measured. Plus, via inspection of the customer sessions within a tool like LogRocket or any other customer session tool, the qualitative impact can be assessed as well. Degradation to the site performance becomes immediately visible.

Another approach is to establish a correlation between your application performance management (APM) alert and a customer session analytics tool.

In this example, let's assume an alert is triggered from New Relic, an APM tool. As your trusted APM tool is alerting you of a critical malfunction, you need to take a piece of information from the alert that could identify customer sessions over to the customer session analytics tool. This can be done manually but is preferably done automatically through an integration.

Such an automatic correlation can be set up between New Relic and FullStory, for example. Once the integration is in place, when alerted by a trace span containing errors, view the customer session that exemplifies the error by watching the representative session(s) in FullStory. Per FullStory's guidance, the integration lets you

> zoom out to understand the broader impact that issue might have on your user base.
>
> —FullStory, *Get the most out of FullStory + New Relic*

It also lets you

> zoom back in on individual sessions to see how each user's experience differed to determine exactly why some users experienced an issue and others did not.
>
> —FullStory, *Get the most out of FullStory + New Relic*

When it is ascertained that some users experienced an issue based on the errors received during the trace span, capture the observed error condition and events surrounding the error and query FullStory in their search interface to determine how many customers were impacted in your application.

Armed with this information, a determination regarding the criticality of the issue can be made and compared against a criticality matrix or service-level commitments. Such a comparison then informs the engineer if the situation needs immediate attention or how the situation stacks up against competing priorities or situations of the moment.

To illustrate what's needed here, Figure 6-19 illustrates signals in relation to impact and noise. Let's assume the graph tracks errors (one of the four golden signals) over time. Any modern SaaS platform will naturally emit errors, but not all of them impact customers to the level that an engineer needs to fix the issue.

Once the error signals impacting customers are understood and tracked as in Figure 6-19, it is reasonable to tie the occurrence of a customer-impacting error to a PagerDuty alert informing an engineer of the existence of the issue. Additionally, it would benefit the engineer to understand the impact level and thus the severity of the issue up front.

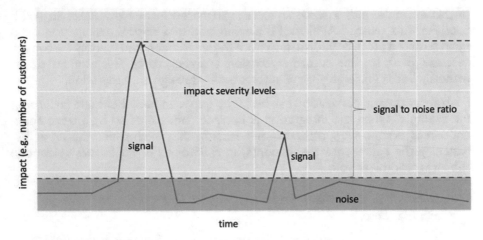

Figure 6-19. Signal and noise

As illustrated in Figure 6-19, the scenario on the left had a higher impact than the scenario on the right. Of course, the system would trigger an alert immediately once the red dotted line is crossed. At that point, it is understood that an engineer needs to take a look. Updated alerts regarding impact to customers would inform the engineer of the severity level, which might trigger different service-level agreements (SLAs) and protocols.

Speed Up RCA (Root Cause Analysis)

Once alerting and customer impact correlation are in place, it becomes imperative to help out with speeding up the root cause analysis so that the impact duration is as short as possible. Any investment into positively improving the time-to-recover metric pays off by increasing the availability of engineering time to devote to value creation vs. fixing broken items.

While customer observability tools increasingly add features that expose JavaScript errors or network latencies or other forms of technical friction, this might be helpful in understanding digital customer experience friction points of technical nature, but they merely form a starting point in the investigation.

Most error situations are more complex, especially in distributed systems. Thus, true high fidelity in customer experience observability is achieved when not only the symptom or customer end point of the experience disturbance is understood but also the complex trace to the root cause. Only when the root cause is genuinely understood, a satisfactory and permanent fix can be deployed.

The callout here is to not stop at observability and visualization of customer experience issues at the UI layer. The idea is to go deeper and to join the DevOps observability efforts by adopting standards and practices allowing for quicker root cause analysis in two directions:

- A technical issue was discovered via UI observability and now needs to be traced through the technology stack.

- An alert occurred deep in the SaaS technology stack, and the alerted engineer wonders about the customer impact.

We covered the second scenario in the previous chapter. Here, we will focus on the first point.

The tools and techniques mentioned here will certainly help with establishing bidirectional traceability and observability.

In her talk on the topic of observability at the GitHub Universe 2020 conference, Christine Yen, the cofounder and CEO of honeycomb.io, explains the "superpowers" developers gain by adopting observability practices.

Christine Yen describes the "second wave" of DevOps as "teaching devs to own code in production" through observability. I encourage watching her presentation *Observability: superpowers for developers* on YouTube or on the GitHub Universe's web page.

Honeycomb has provided an environment (turn to: `www.honeycomb.io/play`) that lets you play with scenarios for hands-on realization of the benefits coming from a professional observability system.

Ownership of code in production requires the technical team to navigate from the issue symptom to its root cause quickly. If they can't do this quickly, other work won't get done or the issue doesn't get addressed in time. Unnecessary frustration builds up, on the engineering team side, and with the impacted customers as well. It is therefore important to get started.

One way of getting started might be to adopt OpenTelemetry:

> *An observability framework for cloud-native software. OpenTelemetry is a collection of tools, APIs, and SDKs. You use it to instrument, generate, collect, and export telemetry data (metrics, logs, and traces) for analysis in order to understand your software's performance and behavior.*

> —opentelemetry.io, *OpenTelemetry*

Lightstep, for example, cofounded OpenTelemetry and provides solutions making instrumentation and observability easier.

In their words

> *Instrumentation shouldn't be a four-letter word.*
>
> —Lightstep, *OpenTelemetry Launchers*

You might also want to check your company's APM tool. Chances are that they are providing solutions for tracing based on the OpenTelemetry concept:

- Datadog embraces OpenTelemetry. Ilan Rabinovitch describes the concept in the article "The future of tracing is open" in Datadog's blog section.

- Dynatrace proudly discusses "Automated, intelligent observability with out-of-the-box OpenTelemetry support" in their Integrations section.

- New Relic's approach is discussed in John Watson's and Lavanya Chockalingam's article "OpenTelemetry: Future-Proofing Your Instrumentation" in New Relic's blog section.

To sum this up, speeding up root cause investigation, perhaps via OpenTelemetry, allows technical teams to focus their efforts on building delightful digital experiences. They are able to quickly react to customer experience issues through crystal clear observability into their distributed systems.

When such an observability system is in place, the DCXE can focus on monitoring for customer friction issues in the knowledge that the teams supporting the DCXE's effort will be as expedient as possible discovering the root cause of any experience disturbance.

Make Customer Experience Friction Monitoring Easy with Dashboards

The word "dashboard" was used multiple times as a device for you to imagine a central place that you can go to where customer friction is highlighted and presented for immediate actioning.

In this section, we will review how to set up a tangible dashboard that provides a one-page or even one-glance pane allowing you to quickly decide if you need to take action on behalf of customers or if everything is working as envisioned and with high quality and fidelity.

The examples reviewed here stem from dashboards featured in online documentation from FullStory, LogRocket, Quantum Metric, and Tealeaf, respectively. They were picked to show the various approaches to creating customer experience–centric dashboards.

Customer Experience Dashboard Example – FullStory

FullStory's dashboard in Figure 6-20 represents a dashboard tracking the user frustration in a purchase funnel. The technique used in this dashboard combines an error graph with four tiles that are changing color depending on certain trigger values.

Figure 6-20. FullStory dashboard example

The spike in the error graph makes the frustrated customer user actions immediately visible. At one glance, it is possible to see that something is not right.

The takeaway here is to summarize business-critical areas in a very concise way, making issues immediately obvious. Any work toward fixing the issues must have a positive impact on the customer experience and the business.

Customer Experience Dashboard Example – LogRocket

LogRocket's dashboard in Figure 6-21 focuses on the system performance to indicate how many customers are frustrated and provides various system performance monitors to showcase where the frustration could stem from. In the example, transactions take longer than five seconds.

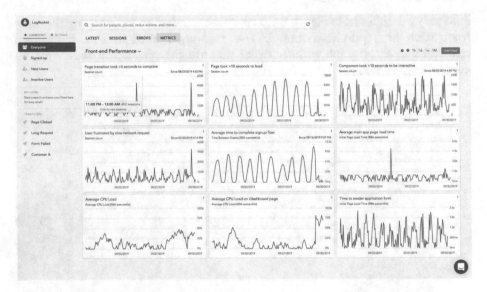

Figure 6-21. LogRocket dashboard example

The dashboard makes it immediately clear that there are frustrated customers by tracking "Users frustrated by slow network requests" and inviting the engineers to investigate the root cause.

The dashboard in Figure 6-21 is discussed in Ben Edelstein's article "Rethinking frontend APM." He summarizes LogRocket Metrics section's benefit by saying

> *LogRocket Metrics ties together session replay and APM in an easy-to-use dashboarding tool that anyone on your team can use, regardless of technical ability.*

Customer Experience Dashboard Example – Quantum Metric

Quantum Metric's dashboard as shown in Figure 6-22 is an example of a dashboard monitoring the purchase flow via a collection of graphs and tiles.

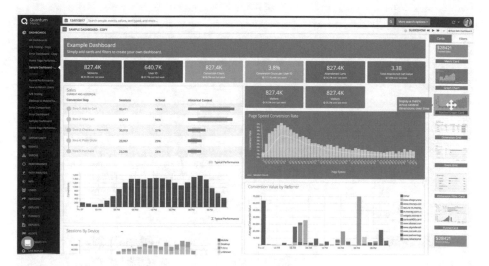

Figure 6-22. Quantum Metric dashboard example

The conversion step graph makes it immediately clear which flow is being monitored. It's the five-step flow starting with Add to Cart and ending with Purchase. The number of sessions metric is paired with historical context graphs, allowing the person looking at the dashboard to immediately detect if something is off.

The tiles above the monitored flow underline the urgency and focus area of investigation. In this case, the abandoned cart value is up by over 100% with a value of over 3.3B. It is not clear which currency was used, but in most currencies 3.3B represent a value promising the people who take action that there is a positive outcome on the other side of completing changes designed to turn the abandoned carts into purchases.

Customer Experience Dashboard Example – Acoustic

Acoustic's experience analytics product is named Tealeaf. It features

> *AI powered struggle analytics.*
>
> —Acoustic, *Experience Analytics (Tealeaf) – Products*

The struggle analytics are being displayed on their struggle detection dashboard as illustrated in Figure 6-23.

Figure 6-23. Acoustic Tealeaf struggle detection dashboard example

The dashboard makes it very clear that there is an issue in the checkout area with 39.5% of the visitors struggling. Again, diving into the issues and detecting the root cause will most likely have a positive impact on the customer experience and the revenue flow.

With a varied sample of dashboards from different vendors on display, my hope is to inspire you to create your own dashboard either by yourself or in conjunction with your DCXE. The dashboard will supply you with focus and will allow for decisive action should the vital indicators turn out to indicate negative experiences on the customers' side.

Seed Your Regression Tests with Customer Journey Interactions

With the collected information about funnel performance and customer journey path experiences, the DCXE can contribute toward making regression tests that are run pre-release more accurate and aligned with real customer interactions.

To do so, the DCXE collects representative sessions that successfully complete a certain customer journey path which is desired to be represented in the regression suite. The goal is to export the HAR files associated with the captured sessions.

> *The HTTP Archive format, or HAR, is a JSON-formatted archive file format for logging of a web browser's interaction with a site.*
>
> —Wikipedia, *HAR (file format)*

As such, it includes all customer interactions with the site. In other words, it includes all the necessary test steps needed for starting the development of regression tests.

The HAR files can be easily exported, for example, via FullStory. Figure 6-24 shows the download location.

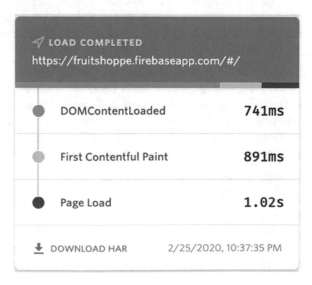

Figure 6-24. HAR file location in FullStory

> *Alongside the page speed metrics for each page loaded within a session, you can also view the Network for more details or download the HAR file that corresponds to the page.*
>
> —FullStory, *Page Speed Metrics*

The next step is to inspect the HAR file with a viewer, for example, the Google Admin Toolbox HAR Analyzer.

Armed with the request and response sequence of the captured sessions, it is now possible to recreate a regression test.

There are also techniques available to convert HAR files into load tests via Gatling.io or other load testing tools.

The preceding discussion creates an opportunity for the DCXE to collaborate with the engineer in charge of test engineering. The goal of the collaboration is to arrive at a customer-centric test methodology that's covering actual customer scenarios.

Speed Up the Analysis of Customer Feedback Received via the Support Channel

For engineers interested in knowing more about customer experience feedback, I recommend reading through the customer support cases associated with a project, product, or feature. While this is typically very insightful, it can be very tiring if there is a large user base involved with thousands of support cases.

Of course, there is a quick-win approach by just reading one or two cases per support topic. That's exactly the approach I recently took when confronted with over 9000 annual issues across 20 topics. Reading through 20–40 items was definitely doable and gave me a good start when working with the respective team. We quickly came up with approaches to tackle the customer experience issues by at least finding one solution path per topic.

While this approach provides a quick path to action, it is lacking, as it is nonsystematic and not very deep.

What's needed is the ability to read through all of the thousand issues while understanding the key issues and the key sentiments of the feedback providers. Now, doing just that on top of their day job is just not feasible for any engineering team member interested in improving the customer feedback.

A solution to this conundrum is to turn to keyword extraction with NLP (natural language processing). This is very helpful as the machine is very patient, will read through the thousands of customer feedback items, and will provide structured information, for example, in the form of a word cloud, that allows for quick assessment of the hot topics.

At a financial services company, I was lucky to have worked with a very talented data science engineer who utilized Python NLP libraries to provide the word cloud and structured keyword clusters that we pre-identified as belonging to specific project-related topics. With her structured report, I was able to gain knowledge of a project's key issues within ten minutes! Before the report, it took me a full week of reading through the issues to understand where the quality issues came from. Naturally, the report became quite popular with other engineers and engineering managers who were interested to get a quick overview with the additional ability to divide and conquer the issues.

Andy Fitzgerald describes how to go about setting up such a system.

> *The output of this process is intended to give you a set of data points you can use to better understand the user feedback contained in large, unstructured data sets. It should also help you more easily focus future analysis and research activities.*

> —Andy Fitzgerald, "Keyword Extraction
> with NLP: A Beginner's Guide"

If you are an AWS user, I recommend you look into Amazon Comprehend.

> *Amazon Comprehend uses natural language processing (NLP) to extract insights about the content of documents.*

> —Amazon, *Amazon Comprehend Developer Guide*

Such insights are "key phrases" and other valuable information. The developer guide includes a tutorial that allows you to practice the benefit of Amazon Comprehend with a time investment of as little as one hour.

Of course, there are prerequisites to meet and certain work needed to adapt this to your specific needs. In any case, this sounds like the ideal topic for a customer experience–themed hackathon.

In fact, I had a chance to work with a very talented group of engineers (Chloe McAteer, Angela Lappin, and Sorcha McNamee) to experiment with Amazon Comprehend during a hackathon in February 2021.

The details are discussed in the article "Comprehending your customer support queue with AWS" (McAteer, Lappin, McNamee, and Wiedenhoefer, 2021) on Medium.

During the hackathon, we exported samples of the NPS comments and other samples of support queues. It was too much information for us to read in detail. We understood some of the feedback, but wanted to understand more, independent of language barriers and the amount of feedback received.

When we exported data from the NPS feedback collection tool, in this case Qualtrics, and the customer service support tool, in this case Salesforce, we noticed that the exported data is not immediately in the format that's perfect for Amazon Comprehend to consume and analyze. So, be aware that a script needs to get written to clean up the information received.

Why go through this trouble? It's a one-time setup that has benefits to the engineers undertaking the work.

> As an engineer with product delivery time pressures, how can we still be customer oriented and empathetic to their needs?
>
> —McAteer, Lappin, McNamee, Wiedenhoefer,
> "Comprehending your customer support queue with AWS"

Let's stay with this interest at the moment, as this is a key statement that this book is trying to highlight. We are looking at two software engineers (Chloe McAteer and Angela Lappin), who are working with their DCXE Sorcha McNamee and other engineers delivering customer-facing software every sprint. This team produces over 40 deployments per week and is very customer focused. They prefer to work on features that delight their customers and invest time to validate and monitor their work, customer experience included.

Spending time to write a cleanup script to add the outputs to Amazon Comprehend was an effort they were willing to do for the promised gain. When Chloe, Angela, and Sorcha worked on setting up the Amazon Comprehend pipeline needed to gain results, it took them not even one day to do so, which included writing a JavaScript cleanup script, uploading the output into S3, and processing the S3 file with AWS Glue as an ETL service for further processing in AWS Athena as the query service that we utilized to enable visualization in AWS QuickSight.

Figure 6-25 illustrates this flow.

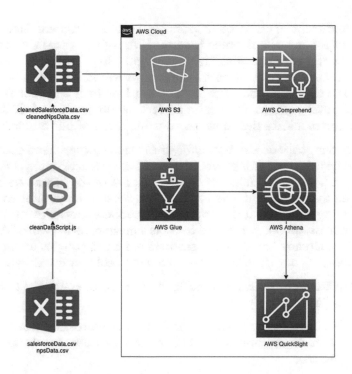

Figure 6-25. *Amazon Comprehend flow from input to visualization*

Please note that we didn't mix the Salesforce or NPS data in the input file. We processed them separately.

On the second day of the hackathon, we analyzed the data and worked on refining the cleanup script to improve the results and wrote the documentation that led to the published article.

We found the sentiment analysis provided by Comprehend quite insightful. We were able to compare the sentiment from the NPS comments against the NPS rating and found this extra level of feedback very helpful.

When we analyzed the support queue sample, we expected only neutral or negative sentiment as people typically turn to support to voice their concerns. We wanted to find out how many people were deeply concerned vs. being just neutral. When we ran the sentiment analysis, we noticed that about 11% of the analyzed feedback sample included positive sentiment! The other part of the sentiment was evenly distributed between neutral and negative. This sparked our interest as we saw this as an opportunity to keep tracking this metric over time. The typical goal would be to decrease the number of concerns, and now we would be also able to track the sentiment composure where we could have the goal to collaborate with support, client services, and our product owner to decrease the negative sentiment and increase the positive sentiment. This is quite possible as the sentiment indicators are basically reflections of customer friction. Filtering the cases that reflect the negative sentiment provides target points for customer experience improvements. If the root cause is technically oriented, our engineers are very motivated to champion the customer and work on fixes and improvements. If there are other reasons for the imperfect sentiment, our DCXE has the means to communicate the concerns to other areas of our business.

Of course, our goal was also to identify if Amazon Comprehend could help us with identifying keywords that would provide us with actionable paths toward enhancing experiences. Sadly, this didn't work out of the box as we expected. We learned that we would have had to write another input filter to filter out high-frequency words that do not have a specific experience meaning. The phrase "your issue" was presented to us as a meaningful keyword. Well, that's true. But we already know that customers are contacting us about an issue, and the phrase "your issue" stemmed from the reply on the ticket.

We quickly learned that we wanted to do two extra steps, time permitting, after the hackathon:

1. Write a filter to exclude high-frequency words and words that do not discuss key experiences that are meaningful to us.

2. Explore the power of the topic analysis feature of Amazon Comprehend.

After the hackathon, we received interest in working on further steps as the benefits of the approach became interesting to others.

For example, the sales department turned to us to find out if we could productionize the sentiment analysis. This would help them to get an additional indicator or early warning sign if a customer might churn. It could also provide an opportunity for the customer success team to reach out to the customer if the sentiment turns to prevent a churn. And it could definitely provide the product owner in conjunction with the UX designer with a tool to analyze workflows or customer journey paths impacted by negative sentiment.

This discussion of Amazon Comprehend hopefully lets you ask yourself and your organization: "How positive is your support queue sentiment?"

Figure 6-26 shows the answer for the sample we analyzed. Surprisingly, the answer was 11% as earlier mentioned. What will be your answer and what are you going to do with this positive insight? Will it drive you to improve your customer experience and experiment with Amazon Comprehend or related tools?

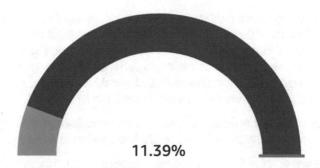

11.39%

Figure 6-26. QuickSight visualization of positive sentiment in support queue

Or, you might say, well, the idea is great, but we don't have the resources to experiment with Amazon Comprehend.

There's still a path for you and your team to pursue insights by experimenting with a SaaS vendor platform. You could turn to a vendor such as SupporTrends. Per their website, they offer sentiments and insights via natural language analysis "from support tickets, online reviews, call recordings, and even surveys."

Figure 6-27 illustrates how SupporTrends' dashboard provides insights from the support queue in a visually attractive and easy to understand way. Understanding the trends via such a dashboard is much quicker and can guide the reader of the dashboard quickly to the details that matter most.

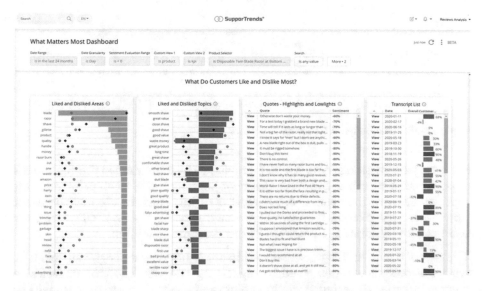

Figure 6-27. Example of a dashboard providing customer support insights via NLP

The goal of the methods described earlier is of course to provide quick insights into hot topics and to zero in on undesirable customer experience scenarios among thousands of feedback items, to track them over time for improvement in the overall customer experience, and to make this process expedient enough so that engineers and product owners can take action before issues manifest themselves into churning customers.

Another way to speed up the analysis of customer feedback is by linking the customer feedback provider's input to their experience session.

Let's say you are involved in an important support topic that was escalated to you, and you need to get to the core of the customer experience issue quickly. A direct link between the tool that captures the customer feedback (perhaps Zendesk or Salesforce or even Pendo or Qualtrics) and the tool capturing the customer experience (e.g., FullStory, sessionstack, LogRocket, Quantum Metric, or Clicktale) is highly desirable. Let's examine how so.

> When an issue arises in your NPS, you can use FullStory to explore the actual digital experiences of your customers.
>
> —Amy Ellis, "Fix friction faster with FullStory & Pendo"

Figure 6-28 shows the information about the hypothetical customer "user-1234" of the hypothetical firm "TestAccount, Inc." in Pendo with the direct link to the most recent FullStory session that recorded the customer's experience.

AGENT	
ID	user-1234
Account	TestAccount, Inc.
language	en_US
mostRecentFullStorySession	https://app.fullstory.com/ui/MYF2J/session/

Figure 6-28. Link between Pendo and FullStory

Following the session allows you to immediately be immersed in the customer's experience. You can see the most recent session and also all prior sessions that line up with the case. From here, it is rather quick to identify the exact time when, for example, an error message showed up or a 404 error, for example, interrupted the progress of the customer's session.

The aim of the preceding discussion is to show how exceedingly tangible it is, with the techniques described, to speed up the detection of undesirable digital customer experience friction points and to shorten the time it takes to turn around the experience from undesirable to delightful.

Implement the Idea of Success Criteria

When it comes to detecting undesirable customer experience issues, the best time to do so is when a new feature is to be released. The concept of release success criteria can help with ensuring early on that digital customer experiences are released well and with the positive desired impact they were designed to deliver.

Let's work on understanding what success criteria are and how they differ from acceptance criteria.

Most engineering teams are already familiar with the concept of acceptance criteria.

Let's look at a definition of acceptance criteria:

> *Acceptance Criteria are a set of statements, each with a clear pass/fail result, that specify both functional and non-functional requirements, and are applicable at the Epic, Feature, and Story Level. Acceptance criteria constitute our "Definition of Done", and by done I mean well done.*

> —Steve Povilaitis, *Acceptance Criteria*

In other words, acceptance criteria define the criteria by which the software development team assesses if the product was built right, meaning built per specification. They are typically evaluated at the end of the agile "Plan-Code-Build-Test" cycle prior to the rollout to production.

Acceptance criteria do not measure, however, if a product was successfully rolled out to production and accepted by the customers. That's where success criteria come in. Success criteria are post-release focused measures with the aim to ascertain release success. After the agile "Plan-Code-Build-Test" cycle, they fit in with the "Release-Deploy-Operate-Monitor" cycle and are evaluated as soon as the release goes live.

> *The success criteria captures what we need to observe and monitor once the product has been released. They include clear metrics and measures that we as a product development team can review after an agreed period of time. These are defined before we release the product to production, and we may use existing measures and metrics as a benchmark.*

> —Aisling McGibbon, "Acceptance Criteria vs Success Criteria: What's the difference?"

Success criteria might aim to answer the following questions:

- Did the release meet the business goal?

- Is the release technically and functionally sound and does it contribute to site stability and availability?

- Was the desired user engagement achieved within the desired timeframe?

- Did the release receive positive user feedback?

- Is the release void of any discernible user experience friction?

Figure 6-29 illustrates the scope of acceptance criteria vs. success criteria.

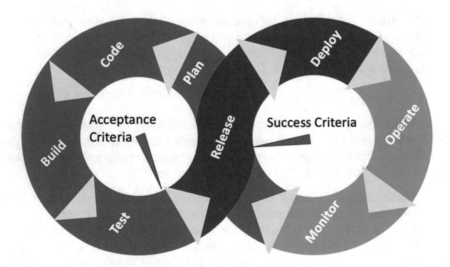

Figure 6-29. Acceptance criteria vs. success criteria

The acceptance criteria are relevant for the cycle from planning through testing. The criteria are developed during this work cycle and are put to the test at the end of the testing period where they might be validated via a demo to the product owner. The success criteria are part of the release cycle and are typically validated through monitoring of the release from the point of deployment throughout the life in production.

Customer experience observability tools and techniques make it increasingly easier to measure the success criteria. Let's discuss a couple of examples for the success criteria questions proposed earlier. At the same time, we will discover how to apply the digital customer experience observability techniques discussed in prior chapters.

Did the Release Meet the Business Goal?

This is a very broad question, and there are, of course, a myriad of approaches to measure the attainment of the business goal. The goal here is to discuss a few examples of measurement.

When starting with success criteria, it is a good idea to have a customer experience dashboard available which can be consulted to verify the success criteria. The article "Dashboards – Overview" by FullStory provides inspiration and guidance regarding the setup.

Let's utilize the first two examples from the article to illustrate the point of measuring if a release met the business goal.

Let's say the business goal of the latest release was to improve the placement of certain items that should result in an increased cart value. If the customer experience dashboard includes a tile like in Figure 6-30 tracking the average cart value, it is possible to understand how the cart value might change over time. The goal might say that the cart value will increase due to some seasonal promotions timed in conjunction with the software release. It might be specific about the percentage of increase.

Figure 6-30. Customer experience dashboard tile tracking cart value

With a tile tracking the average cart value and the direction of the value (in the example, minus 91% prior to the release), it is now possible to see the impact of the release. The color shows the positive impact of the release so far. The engineering team should get with the product owner to be very specific about the measuring timeframe and the specific metrics. FullStory allows these measures to translate into colors representing the goals. If they are not attained, the color changes to yellow or perhaps red.

The other very fitting example for discussing measuring business results is illustrated in Figure 6-31, which tracks the conversion rate of the checkout flow.

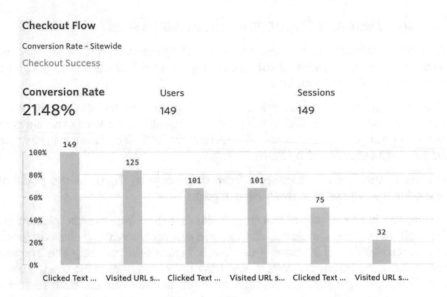

Figure 6-31. Customer experience dashboard tile tracking the conversion rate

If the goal of the release was to implement features that improve the conversion rate by a certain percentage, this tile on the dashboard is essential to visualize release success. Again, a color would be helpful. Let's say the conversion rate above 21% was the business goal. The tile should be coded to be green in color so that it is clear with one glance if a goal was met or not.

Is the Release Technically and Functionally Sound and Does It Contribute to Site Stability and Availability?

In other words, this question includes the aspects of a software feature that works, is void of errors, and is available to the customer.

Breaking this down into its components, the first question is about finding out if the feature actually works. To attempt the measure here, it is a good idea to understand the experience flow of the implemented feature and the events contributing to the desired experience. The interaction points and events (perhaps positive feedback events that lead to the next necessary interaction in the experience path) can be illustrated via a flow chart similar to the one illustrated in Figure 6-31. This requires a discussion with the product owner to estimate how many customers who are engaging with a certain feature should be able to successfully complete the flow.

Let's say the answer is 100% of customers who are engaging with a flow should be able to successfully complete the flow. If you experience a value of 86%, showing that 14% of your users can't be successful, you have an immediate issue. A tile on the customer experience dashboard turning red will immediately alert the team that there is an issue. Is this example hypothetical? Sadly, it is not, as this exact scenario happened when I worked with a team looking at their release success. They noticed that there was a production use case the team was not able to envision up front. When they observed the sessions within the struggling customer segment, they immediately noticed the missing property they didn't know the customer could possess. They were able to fix the situation before any customer was able to submit any experience issue. Believe me, I checked. They were really quick! This quickness of reaction is what you are aiming for. That's why you implement success criteria.

Of course, the implemented feature should be void of errors that impact the customer experience. We should welcome error messages that meaningfully guide the customer toward success. What we don't want to tolerate are errors that just interrupt the flow and prevent the customer from completing their experience or just delay their efforts. My favorite error I don't want to see again is "please try again later." Shouldn't the feature work in the first place, not later, but now? To help answer this rhetorical question, employ your favorite error monitoring tool to understand the impact of errors to the user experience.

Techniques regarding the metric of the *error rate* are discussed later in the chapter discussing key metrics to consider. The key point here is to ensure that the customer experience–impacting errors are kept to the absolute minimum possible following a release. Ideally, there is zero. And ideally the team is set up to understand the impact of the errors that do surface. Knowing the degree of impact on the customers overall or a certain customer segment helps to determine next steps quickly. Should we pull the release or add the issue to the tech debt to be fixed as soon as possible and warranted by the intensity of the impact compared against the business value realized by the implementation so far.

The last, but not least, part of the question posed earlier for ascertaining release success was to ensure the feature is available to the customer. For an answer to this question, I would look at the uptime metric and Apdex score of your system. These two metrics are discussed later in the section "Other Customer Experience KPIs to Consider" in Chapter 7. This is a callout to employ these metrics as tools for success criteria evaluation.

Was the Desired User Engagement Achieved Within the Desired Timeframe?

A great example of how to answer this question at the time of the release is illustrated by Heap Analytics in their discussion of *Engagement*.

Figure 6-32 picks up the example showcased on their page for the illustration of measuring success criteria.

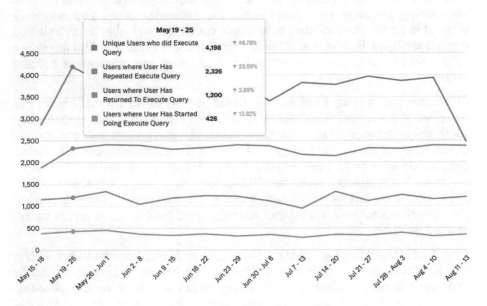

Figure 6-32. Engagement tracking in Heap Analytics

Let's say the engineering team worked on the feature "Execute Query." The graph featured by Heap Analytics and reflected in Figure 6-32 tracks the success the customers have with the feature. Using such a graph is instrumental as the release should not negatively impact the customer experience, but instead enhance it. So, tracking engagement over time pays off when measuring for release success.

Did the Release Receive Positive User Feedback?

Direct feedback right after the release from real users inside the digital experience of the app or feature you just deployed would be desirable in order to answer this question. The technique that helps answering this question directly is to use your customer experience tools for in-app feedback collection strategically.

An article illustrating this point is published by the Pendo Help Center:

> *Now, Pendo and Qualtrics give you the power to bring surveys right where your customers live, in your app. Data shows it's possible to get higher response rates when customers are in the moment.*
>
> —Pendo, "Qualtrics: Increase your Survey Response Rate by Bringing it Into Your App"

When a survey like this is set up, it is possible to make a quick assessment of the customers' opinions after the release. It could be in a quick fashion of just asking if a new feature was helpful or not.

At time of release, it is very critical to retrieve customer feedback in the moment. Even if your organization is not using Qualtrics XM and Pendo, it is still beneficial to understand the setup and to think how your organization could follow this idea.

Regardless which tool you are ending up using, you want feedback from the customer at the time of the experience, not later.

Is the Release Void of Any Discernible User Experience Friction?

The next component to discuss is about the engineering team measuring common friction points with the release of the feature.

We discussed the techniques of identifying rage clicks, dead clicks, error clicks, form abandonment, and thrashing mouse customer experience issues in the section "Detect and Remove Customer Friction." This is a callout to employ the techniques from that chapter in your success criteria. It could be as simple as saying that no additional friction elements should occur after a release.

Outside of customer friction, your success criteria should include the stated goal of no net new errors after the release. You might already have a system that emits errors, and you are working hard to pair this down. You definitely want to shut the door to the possibility of leaking and introducing new errors.

Linking your error management tool to your source code tool might be a solution for detection of errors right after a release. The GitHub and Sentry integration provide an example of how to integrate the two. Via this integration, the Sentry errors can then be filtered by version identifiers from GitHub, and new errors emanating from the newly deployed code are quickly becoming visible after a release goes live. For more details, refer to the article "GitHub" in the Sentry documentation.

Another path to identifying user experience friction points might be to employ crowd testing right before and after the release. My current organization has experience surfacing customer experience issues via the services of Applause, a crowd testing service provider. There's of course test.io and others who are active in this space. I've seen value in services of crowd testing as they are actively surfacing friction elements that we are currently not able to detect via other means.

Summary Regarding Success Criteria

Now that we discussed a variety of possible questions and techniques for assessing release success criteria, it is time to call out that teams implementing software features should consider the preceding points for each release. Acceptance criteria should include the point that success criteria are selected, defined, implemented as monitors, and measurable. The combination of acceptance and success criteria enhances the quality of a product, and the close evaluation of both enhances the likelihood of release success.

The DCXE should work with the product owner and the engineering team to ensure the conversations around success criteria are happening and that appropriate measures are available in the observability tools to ascertain success.

Customer Observability and Privacy Considerations

> *Privacy is not something that I'm merely entitled to, it's an absolute prerequisite.*
>
> —Marlon Brando, Actor

More and more customers agree with Marlon Brando. Privacy is not just a nice-to-have feature but a prerequisite, even a right. With privacy being the prerequisite and even right that your customers expect to be in place and maintained during their interaction with your digital product or service, you need to ensure that any customer experience observability practice and tooling the DCXE puts in place adheres to the best privacy practices.

Being compliant with all important laws and regulations is critical here. This doesn't only apply to the processes and tooling of your company. It applies to the tooling you are purchasing from the software vendors you contract to enable customer experience observability. And it also applies to how you are going to incorporate the tooling into your privacy-informed information system to enable the practices demanded by law.

Let me explain this point as it sometimes gets overlooked. Your company might be CCPA (California Consumer Privacy Act) compliant, an important California privacy regulation. The vendor might be CCPA compliant, and their tooling has CCPA-compliant features. My point here is, if you don't spend effort into understanding how to hook up the CCPA-compliant features into your company's CCPA compliance practices, you will fail to be CCPA compliant and are opening a huge risk to your company.

Let's say this again in positive language: when you select a tool that is compliant with all the modern privacy regulations needed in your sector and area of operation, you will spend the time and effort needed to install the information stream needed to make the tool you just purchased compliant with the law and regulation.

This is actually not as exhausting as it sounds. Modern tools make this as easy as possible. They have sections dedicated in their online documentation on how to ensure you are not recording PII (personally identifiable information) data. They also provide assistance in understanding complicated regulations such as GDPR or CCPA, to name a few, and the work that's needed to comply with these regulations.

Let's go through a few examples.

In the online documentation of sessionstack, a session recording tool, you will find the following passage:

We're have already built features that are needed for the GDPR:

> *Ability to discard IP addresses and exclude them through our UI.*
>
> *Ability to delete an individual within our UI.*
>
> *Retroactive deletion of specific field captures.*
>
> *Flexible monitoring mechanisms that give you control over the types of traffic and users that you want to be monitoring.*
>
> *Opt-out for end users.*
>
> —sessionstack, GDPR

Their page guides you through your responsibilities and how to work through them, covering the steps you need to take and which assistance the company and their tool provide.

Another example covers the CCPA. When you look up the term *California Consumer Privacy Act (CCPA) and FullStory* on FullStory's Learning Center online, you will find a detailed walk-through of what you need to know regarding the

CCPA, guidance to find out if the regulation applies to your business, what it requires, and many more detailed tips to ensure the tool is set up correctly with a full degree of compliance.

I mentioned earlier that staying compliant and conforming to privacy requests from your customers does not have to be complicated when using a customer experience tool such as a session recording tool. FullStory again provides an example reflected in Figure 6-33.

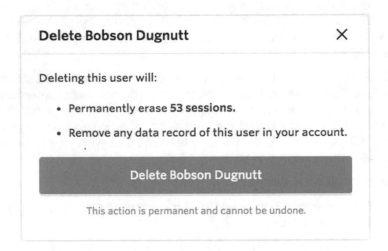

Figure 6-33. Deleting a user for compliance purposes in FullStory

If a customer requests that their recorded information is deleted via the opt-out mechanism (in other words, they exercise their "right to be forgotten"), you have the ability to delete the customer via a dedicated "delete user" button. And if manual deletion is not efficient for your business, they are also offering an API to process the deletion programmatically.

What's important for the DCXE or the person responsible for the customer experience tooling to remember, though, is to contact their privacy and security department's specialist. The goal of the discussion with the privacy and security specialist is to find out how to obtain the feed of information requests, deletion requests, etc. coming from customers exercising their privacy rights.

Another to-do in the conversation with the privacy and security specialist is to ensure your company's privacy notice includes the fact that you are recording the customer's session and what data is recorded and for what purpose. Your company's privacy notice should include at least a passage that says something like "We may use personal data about how you use our products and services to enhance your user experience and to help us diagnose technical and service problems and administer our platform."

If such language or similar language is not included, you have more work to do and should refrain from using session recording or experience tracking tools until the privacy notice is up to date.

Note that the recommendations in this chapter are not an exhaustive list of actions to take. The discussion in this chapter is meant for you, the reader, as a starting point on the topic. It is written to encourage you to complete the due diligence and actions required to make privacy a priority and best practice for your business.

Reflect the Customer Experience Insights to Your Customers

For SaaS B2B (business-to-business) companies that are providing a digital services platform, the practice of digital customer experience engineering means providing a platform experience with a high degree of functional availability and a high degree of functionality, devoid of customer experience issues. Such businesses are routinely collecting information about the platform experience as they are optimizing their platform and adding new capabilities and features.

And, to the advantage of their customers and the end consumer, they provide insights that guide improvements and customer adoption of new features or experiences.

Let's look at the example of Pendo. They are providing a tool named Pendo Adopt. Adopt helps their customers provide targeted guidance and education to end users. Let's say you are the end user, and you are struggling to understand a feature, wouldn't you like it if you could receive tailored guidance, enabling you to get back on track as smoothly as possible?

Pendo lists an example on their web page.

> Pendo Adopt helps Q2 give small financial institutions the power of in-app messaging.
>
> —Pendo.io, *Unlock custom in-app training*

The write-up is an interesting account of how Michael Vasquez, a product owner at Q2, is using data points in an anonymized, compliant, and effective way to empower his customers to guide their end users in an effective and secure way.

> *Our customers have been clamoring for the capability to deploy messages, and they've been wanting to understand the usage of their navigation. With Adopt, I don't have to worry about someone going to set up something in the API and accidentally putting in the wrong financial institution number.*
>
> —Michael Vasquez, "Pendo Adopt helps Q2 give small financial institutions the power of in-app messaging"

The guides provided by the platform are compliant, secure, and safe. And they help Q2's customers, small financial institutions, provide messaging to their customers that is on target and on point as they guide their customers through complicated financial products and features.

Q2's example shows how a business platform enables in-app communication to a segment of their customers needing the communication most while enabling their financial platform customers to be aware of their banking customers' needs via usage analytics.

Let's take a look at another example from the ecommerce space.

Bazaarvoice provides their customers with a product called Network Performance Insights. Bazaarvoice is a SaaS platform "connecting thousand of brands and retailers to the voices of their customers." Voices of the customers are expressed via user-generated content (UGC), in the form of reviews, feedback, pictures, and videos describing product experiences.

Bazaarvoice enables their partners to improve upon the customer experience via their Network Performance Insights product. In the article "Network Performance Insights: Maximize the ROI on your ratings and reviews program," Product Marketing Manager Brianna Byers explains the three benefits of the product:

> *Network Performance Insights: which allows you to quickly see how your UGC is doing and where you can improve performance at your retailers.*
>
> *Sentiment Insights: which helps you understand what customers like and dislike about your brand at retail through advanced machine learning and natural language processing.*

Named Competitor Insights: that help you to stay in tune with how your UGC performance and customer sentiment stack up to your competitors.

As you can see, insights from this product are enabling brands to react to customer feedback and sentiment in new ways, improving the overall shopping experience and experience with the products the brands are selling.

The preceding collection of examples is meant as a stimulus for your thinking. How are you going to provide insights to your customers, enabling them to enhance digital experiences?

Build the Foundation for Tracking Customer Experience Engineering Metrics

Later on, in another chapter, we will discuss several key metrics for tracking customer engineering–centric metrics. These metrics are central for keeping an eye on how your effort and focus on customer experience improvements are trending. Chapter 7 will discuss what these metrics are and how they might fit into what you need to track.

In this chapter, we are discussing the underpinnings of the metrics, namely, which kind of information flows you should have set up so that reporting on the customer experience information flow via the essential metrics is as smooth as possible.

Figure 6-34 illustrates the two information flows we will be focusing on:

- The customer experience guidance flow
- The root cause analysis flow

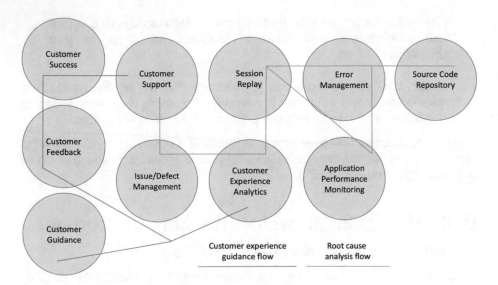

Figure 6-34. End-to-end integrations for experience guidance and root cause analysis

Let's look at the customer experience guidance flow first.

The customer experience guidance flow combines functions of Customer Success, Customer Support, Customer Feedback, and Customer Guidance.

> *Customer Success is the business methodology of ensuring customers achieve their desired outcomes while using your product or service.*
>
> —Gainsight, "Why Every Business Needs Customer Success"

> *Customer Support is a service provided to help customers resolve any technical problems that they may have with a product or service.*
>
> —Collins Dictionary, *Customer Support*

> *Customer Feedback is information provided by customers about their experience with a product or service.*
>
> —Pendo, "What is Customer Feedback"

The basis of successful customer guidance is information. When people get relevant information – more signal, less noise – they feel more relaxed and calm. Customers at ease take their time, are more open to new experiences, and look around more. In the long run, this leads to increased spending.

—tego.se, "The basis of customer guidance: information"

Linking these functions together with essential customer experience information allows these functions to work better together and improve their inherent efficiencies on their own and together.

For example, if a customer indicates something is bothering them during an NPS survey (Customer Feedback) and Customer Support has this information at hand, they can better empathize and readily look for a solution. The same is true for Customer Success as they want to be aware of the customer's needs. To stay with this example, let's say the issue was now fixed and the customer logs in again, Customer Guidance could greet the customer by informing them with a message that their feedback was heard and an improvement was delivered.

Next up, we will take a look at the root cause analysis flow.

The root cause analysis flow aims to speed up the identification of the root cause for any given customer experience friction point. It does so by expertly linking information from a customer support issue to the escalated technical issue management software with the customer experience analytics software, arming the engineer with an overview that links the impact of an issue directly to the root cause in the source code management system via application performance monitoring (APM) tracing functionality and linked-in error management overviews.

Modern software development and software management tools are highly connectable via integrations and connections they may provide. They might also support OpenTelemetry or other forms of tracing that have the goal to speed up root cause analysis. There are also other tools available providing connection services if a connector is not provided by the vendor (Tray.io and Automate.io are two examples).

An example of a linked-up root cause analysis flow could be Salesforce Service Cloud linked to the JIRA defect management cloud linked to the customer experience analytics software (Pendo) and the session replay software (FullStory). In this scenario, product owners could see in Pendo how many issues of technical nature are associated with an experience flow. The engineer on the team would be able to prioritize a technical issue by looking at FullStory, Sentry (for error management), and the APM tool (possibly Datadog) to look at the issue nature, impact, and root cause in one glance. Perhaps GitHub is also linked up to the error management tool (in this example, Sentry), which would provide the code view of the issue, while Sentry would also be able to say if the error came from the particular code with the last release while GitHub specifies the commit that is responsible for the issue in the new release, if any, meaning if it wasn't a legacy issue.

Now imagine if these flows are created and linked together. That's modern customer experience management and engineering par excellence. It's a powerful end-to-end information flow that's measurable and easy to visualize. Best of all, it makes it possible to easily verify the business case and the subsequent investment in the customer experience area.

Key Metrics

For successful digital engineering, customer quality, and observability

As we are now fully aware of the techniques employed by the DCXE, we need to provide a foundation of key metrics in the field of customer experience analytics.

In this chapter, we will review the top customer experience metrics most commonly in use.

We will also look at other Key Performance Indicators (KPIs), that is, metrics, providing an engineer with the ability to quickly detect progress made toward improved digital customer experiences.

The list is meant to provide the basics to get started. There are definitely more metrics out there that can be used, and each organization should have a discussion related to the selection and definition of the metrics for their specific needs.

© Lars Wiedenhoefer 2021
L. Wiedenhoefer, *Digital Customer Experience Engineering*,
https://doi.org/10.1007/978-1-4842-7243-5_7

Top Six Customer Experience Metrics for Engineering Teams to Consider

In a blog on Luoma.me, Anna Pogrebniak reviews the "6 Most Popular Customer Experience Metrics and KPIs Explained Simply" which are

- Net Promoter Score (NPS)
- Customer Satisfaction (CSAT)
- Customer Effort Score (CES)
- Churn rate
- Retention rate
- Customer Lifetime Value (CLV)

The preceding metrics stood out from a customer experience survey named *The State of the Customer Experience* Luoma conducted in 2018. From personal experience, the choice of top six resonates with me as the organizations I worked at kept most, if not all, of the metrics for their customer experience considerations.

Let's take a look at them individually.

NPS

We discussed NPS in the section "Customer Success Team" in Chapter 5 briefly and included the definition of the metric.

From a business perspective, NPS is directionally very helpful as it is a good barometer of the overall customer sentiment. Specific questioning can provide insights into further themes of interest.

While the NPS score is directionally interesting, it seldom provides directly actionable insight to the DCXE as the customer provides a score ("how likely are you to recommend our product to a friend or family?") and a brief description that sometimes articulates why the score was given. It is not directly designed to provide specific actionable insights in regard to digital customer experience issues and most always requires further digging into recorded customer sessions or provided comments from focus groups.

The NPS analysis is easier to conduct when the NPS survey is conducted as close as possible to the time of the experience and if the person having the experience provides the NPS feedback. In this case, the DCXE should be able to retrieve possible recorded customer sessions to review what might have gone wrong. In this sense, it is even better if tools link the customer experience directly to the feedback provider. Immediate insight analysis can be conducted when NPS scores dive below an acceptable or desired level.

CSAT

The Customer Satisfaction (CSAT) metric measures the customer satisfaction by asking the customer to provide a rating for a product or service, typically by asking customers to evaluate the product or service "on a scale of 1 to 5" where 5 is the highest value and 1 is the lowest.

We all have the experience of service providers asking us to leave a five-star rating. While this is good directional feedback, for the DCXE there is value in the feedback when the session of the customer experience is captured. If customers consistently provide only two stars, for example, it helps if the DCXE can evaluate the sessions to possibly identify the root cause of the issue. The DCXE's goal is to exclude a technical root cause and to share other observations made from reviewing the sessions.

CES

Similar to the CSAT metric, the Customer Effort Score (CES) asks the customer a simple question, but instead of asking for an overall star rating, the metric tries to ascertain the effort the customer needed to take to get done whatever they tried to get done. It's typically measured on a scale of "difficult" to "easy." For the DCXE, consistent ratings of "difficult" would trigger a search for technical friction within the customers' experience paths.

Churn Rate

Churn rate measures how many customers simply turned away and didn't come back. As customer churn is expensive for any business, it is valuable to track this customer experience metric. It is typically known how much the acquisition of a new customer costs. With this information, it is possible to build a solid business case for the customer observability practice of the DCXE.

Let's look at a possible business case to illustrate the value of the customer experience engineering practice provides to the business. Let's assume an acquisition cost of $100 per customer. Let's further assume regular monthly customer traffic of 140,000 monthly active customers with a churn rate of 20% per month. This will result in a cost of churn of $2.8 million. Meaning $2.8 million would need to be injected monthly to keep the 140,000 monthly actives going.

If the DCXE can show that, for example, 30% of the churn is resulting from technical issues and can work with their team to resolve the underlying issues, this would mean $840,000 of the $2.8 million could be recouped. Well, minus the effort, of course, as it takes effort to fix the issues. Let's say it takes 14 engineering hours to fix an issue on average and there are 20 underlying issues that need to get fixed, and an engineering hour costs $97.50. This means the cost of resolving the issues is $27,300. So, after investing this sum, there's still an $812,700 benefit ($840,000 minus $27,300) to the business by investing the $27,300 in fixing customer experience issues preventing churn.

The cost/benefit analysis should be considered when it comes to assigning work to the engineering team or picking up issues from the backlog to be worked on in upcoming sprints (assuming an agile workflow).

Extra tips for this example on how to come up with the numbers:

Question: How do I calculate what represents 30% of the churn?

Answer: If your business receives 100 customer complaints that can be attributed to the churn, 20 underlying technical issues represent 30% of the churn.

Question: How do I know how long it takes to resolve issues?

Answer: The hours it takes to resolve technical issues on average can be calculated by measuring "time to resolution (TTR)," which is typically measured by measuring the hours between the time an issue got opened and the time it got closed. JIRA or any other issue management tool makes this quite easy to calculate.

Retention Rate

The retention rate is basically the reverse of the churn rate. It measures how many customers are retained vs. are churning. The considerations for retention rate in our context of the book are essentially the same as for the churn rate.

CLV

Customer Lifetime Value (CLV) is a prognostication of the net profit contributed to the whole future relationship with a customer. The prediction model can have varying levels of sophistication and accuracy, ranging from a crude heuristic to the use of complex predictive analytics techniques.

—Wikipedia, *Customer Lifetime Value*

Whatever the level of sophistication used to calculate CLV is quite useful for the business and the DCXE as it can be used to measure the impact of a customer experience issue. Is the impact high enough to materially impact CLV for the customer or a range of customers? Such impact assessments should be utilized to prioritize issues that naturally come up and should be utilized in conjunction with SLAs that define how quickly an issue needs to be fixed if it falls within a certain impact category on an issue classification matrix.

For example, a customer experience issue impacts a customer with a CLV of $100,000, and on the issue classification matrix this CLV issue is associated with a priority of P2, and the SLA for a P2 issue is 15 days. This would mean the engineers have 15 days to fix this issue. This is very helpful when it comes to prioritizing customer experience issues that come up while the engineering team is working on other issues during their agile sprint. Perhaps, the P2 rating doesn't mean that items within the sprint need to be dropped. It might mean that this issue can be considered and prioritized for the next sprint.

Other Customer Experience KPIs to Consider

Beyond the six most popular customer experience metrics, the technical teams need to consider some additional Key Performance Indicators (KPIs). The items to consider should express the health of the customer experience as well as the health of the site serving up the customer experience.

Candidates for engineering KPIs in support of measuring the customer experience are

- Apdex score
- Error rate
- Uptime
- Number of escalated customer experience issues
- Number of detected customer experience issues
- Time to resolution
- SLA adherence
- Number of site incidents
- Software security–related metrics
- Number of success criteria validated

Let's take a look at these additional metrics individually.

Apdex Score

Apdex (Application Performance Index) is an open standard for measuring performance of software applications in computing. Its purpose is to convert measurements into insights about user satisfaction, by specifying a uniform way to analyze and report on the degree to which measured performance meets user expectations.

—Wikipedia, *Apdex*

As it becomes clear from the definition provided by Wikipedia, the Apdex score is an ideal measure for quickly obtaining a glance at the overall customer experience. It focuses on the performance of the site and provides an overview of how many customers are "satisfied," "tolerating," or "frustrated." Apdex is supported by over 30 tools, such as Datadog, Dynatrace, New Relic, Airbrake, and many more.

In his article "How to Choose Apdex T: The Final Word" on the New Relic Blog, Bill Kayser illustrates how Apdex works and how to set the T value, which helps to define the group of customers that are "tolerating" the service being measured.

If you set your alert threshold too low, you're going to be flooded with false alerts, causing the ops team to lose confidence in the alerting system. If you set your alert threshold too high, IT ops could miss relevant performance degradation, resulting in a poor user experience.

—Bill Kayser, "How to Choose Apdex T: The Final Word"

Figure 7-1 illustrates the Apdex example showing the Apdex score concept.

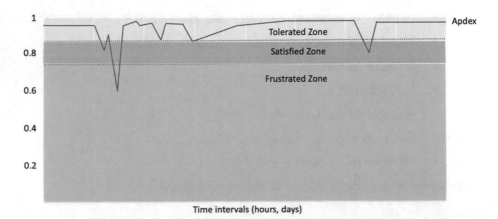

Figure 7-1. Apdex score example

Just in case you are wondering about the T value, it's the time value separating the "tolerating" customer sessions from the "satisfied" ones.

For example, if the T value is set to 300 milliseconds, a response time of less than 300 ms is considered "satisfied," while a longer response time is considered as fitting the "tolerating" segment until it reaches four times T. Above that, the sessions are considered "frustrated." For more details and how to best set the T value, it's paramount to read Bill's article.

In the Apdex example of Figure 7-1, it is very clear to see where and when the dips in the score occurred, which shows the DCXE and the other engineers a clear target for their customer experience issue investigation.

What's noteworthy here is the applicability of the Apdex score as a customer experience measure as it delivers a quantifiable experience score from the browser-side and the server-side perspective at one glance.

Error Rate

Tracking the error rate of your service or application will allow you to identify unusual spikes, valleys, or other erratic patterns of potentially customer-impacting behavior. Once such patterns are detected, they can be analyzed for insights and future prevention.

The error rate measures the rate of errors over the measuring time compared against the total requests that occurred during the time. For example, if you measured your application error rate for the last ten minutes where you recorded 15 errors and 25 transactions, your error rate would be 0.6.

In itself, this number doesn't tell us anything. If only the error rate is looked at, it's good to have a rate as low as possible. Again, abnormal behavior is interesting. Peaks, valleys, and erratic patterns must be looked at.

Modern APM tools let you track the error rate and link errors to your customer experience monitoring setup. When this is set up, for example, via an integration of Sentry.io and FullStory, you can navigate to an error spike in your error management tool and review if there was any customer experience impact. The DCXEs should be able to set this up so that error rate and customer experience issues can be correlated, alerted on, and remedied. In each case, root cause investigations are needed to understand the errors better and mitigate customer impact if any was detected.

Patrick Brandt describes in his article "Understanding React + Redux Errors With Sentry and FullStory" how to utilize the link between Sentry and FullStory to trace React errors. He explains what is needed to install the link between the tools and how to work with the integration.

Once this is set up on both sides, you are able to see the FullStory URL on the Sentry error page beneath the breadcrumbs error trail (Figure 7-2).

Headers

User-Agent	Mozilla/5.0 (Windows NT 10.0; WOW64) AppleWebKit/537.36 (KHTML, like Gecko) Chrome/88.0.4324.146 Safari/537.36

BROWSER

name	Chrome
version	88.0.4324

FULLSTORY

fullStoryUrl	https://app.fullstory.com/ui/ZFBHF/session/4992130119221248%3A6427275420745 728%3A1612905895640 ⬈

OPERATING SYSTEM

Name	Windows

Figure 7-2. FullStory URL in Sentry

After following this link, it is possible to view the session in FullStory and observe within the recorded session if and how the error impacted the customer. Figure 7-3 shows how FullStory calls out the Sentry error in the continuous event stream of actions.

Figure 7-3. Sentry error in FullStory

Within the FullStory recorded session, you also see at the bottom of the recording embedded in the timeline how often Sentry errors surfaced.

Figure 7-4 shows a distribution example, which illustrates three Sentry errors (marked by the thunderbolts) within the recorded session.

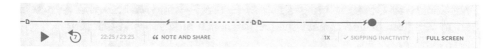

Figure 7-4. Occurrences of Sentry errors within a FullStory recorded session

By marking the Sentry errors in the timeline, the error impact on the customer session at hand is visualized and allows the investigating engineer to quickly wind forward to the sections possibly impacted by the Sentry errors.

While Figure 7-4 described the visualization of Sentry errors within a session, Figure 7-5 looks at how to search in FullStory for the occurrence of Sentry issues across sessions of any user. The illustration shows a global search within the Everyone segment.

Everyone	PAST MONTH ∨	ANY USER · 1 EVENT	SAVE SEGMENT...

USER FILTERS · Find people who match the following characteristics

Any user ∨ + × ⋮

EVENT FILTERS · Find people who performed these events

Custom Event ∨   Sentry Error ∨   ⇄ + × ⋮

Exclude people who performed...

Figure 7-5. FullStory event filter for Sentry errors

Additionally, it might also be beneficial to add the search for Sentry errors to specific segments in order to find out how errors that were caught in Sentry are surfacing in critical customer experience segments.

Once the mapping between the error monitoring and customer experience session software is established, the impact of an error can immediately be observed.

Noisy errors are going to be soon history, and meaningful errors with real impact are welcome as they provide the opportunity to quickly erase customer experience impediments.

If your teams have reached this point of integration and experience insight, it might be also a good idea to go a step further and consider the linking of your error monitoring tool with the application performance monitoring (APM) tool.

The Sentry-to-Datadog integration in Figure 7-6 shows how the errors in Sentry are juxtaposed against the performance indicators in Datadog.

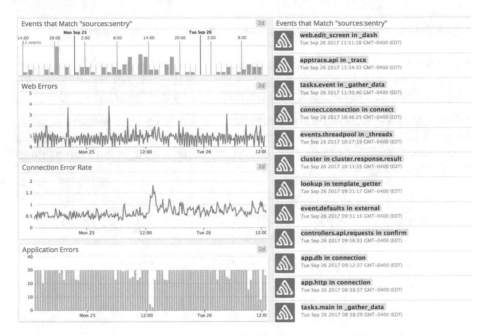

Figure 7-6. Error monitoring and APM combination – a Datadog and Sentry example

Michael Chen explains in his article "Collaborative Bug Fixing with Datadog's Sentry Integration" on the Datadog blog how to set up and best use this integration.

> *Adding the Sentry integration to your Datadog account only takes a few minutes.*
>
> —Michael Chen, "Collaborative Bug Fixing with Datadog's Sentry Integration"

From a DCXE point of view, the value is clear. With an integration of say Sentry to FullStory and Sentry to Datadog, there's a direct path from error to customer experience issue to a clear starting point of investigation in the system via the APM.

From there, it's a small step to integrate the ideas shared in the section "Speed Up RCA (Root Cause Analysis)" in Chapter 6 via tracing to radically accelerate the time from error detection to impact to root cause to resolution (via fixing or mitigating the issue). Keep this in mind as we will be discussing the time to resolution metric later in this chapter.

Uptime

Uptime is a metric that measures the reliability of a system. For a system to be beneficial to customers and their experience, it needs to be there, serving up the customer experience paths and journeys the system was designed to handle. Therefore, systems ideally need to have a 100% uptime. That's of course the ideal. Most uptime goals come in at over 99%.

Let's see what an uptime goal of 99.9% would mean to an organization. There's downtime involved, and that means direct impact to the customer experience! So, how many hours of downtime does this allow for? There are 8760 hours in a year (365 days times 24 hours). To see what 99.9% means in regard to impact to uptime, the following equation will provide the answer: 99.9%*8760 hours = 8751.24 hours. This means a little over 8 hours would be the annual downtime to customers if the uptime goal is 99.9%.

Number of Site Incidents

In addition to measuring uptime, it is a good idea to also keep an eye on the number of site incidents with impact on the uptime metric. Tracking the incidents over time creates good visibility into how many incidents already occurred and how much of the budgeted downtime was already consumed.

In their article "How to choose incident management KPIs and metrics," Atlassian identifies the benefits of tracking the number of site incidents over time:

> Are incidents happening more or less frequently over time? Is the number of incidents acceptable or could it be lower? Once you identify a problem with the number of incidents, you can start to ask questions about why that number is trending upward or staying high and what the team can do to resolve the issue.

Figure 7-7 provides an example of tracking the number of site incidents in conjunction with the uptime goal, actual uptime per month, and the remaining error budget in hours. As the example illustrates, the organization was on track with their error budget up to the month of June. In July, eight issues consumed six hours of impact, nearly depleting the entire error budget for the year. As the organization recovered, there was still further impact in August.

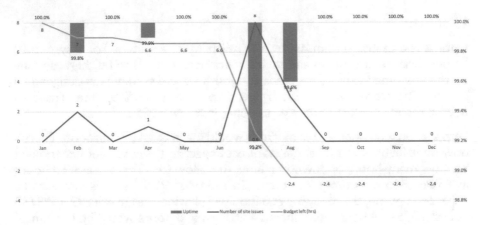

Figure 7-7. Tracking uptime, site incidents, and error budget in hours

While the impact was not as devastating to the customer experience as in July, it nevertheless was felt as it took the site down for and accumulated three hours triggered by three incidents during the month of August. This completely consumed the error budget and then some, driving the organization far away from their goal of 99.9% uptime for the year.

In the example, the engineering organization, to their credit, learned quite a bit from the incidents and applied the lessons learned gathered from the retrospectives and root cause analyses. The impact of their good spirit is evident. While they didn't meet the corporate goal, they still exceeded the monthly goal and achieved 100% uptime over the next four months. Let's hope that this also set them up for a better customer experience and goal attainment the following year.

Number of Escalated Customer Experience Issues

The number of escalated customer experience issues are issues that would typically originate from the support and client success organizations as representatives collecting customer feedback. These tickets contain customer experience concerns. Some of these concerns are technical in nature and indicate that there is something not quite right with the technical systems supporting the customer journey paths.

Support and client success organizations typically refer customer issues of technical nature to the engineering organization for investigation and resolution.

If support and client success cases are recorded, for example, in Salesforce as a customer relationship management tool and technical issues are kept, for example, in JIRA as an error management tool, they can be easily measured as issues in JIRA originating from support or client success and having a link to the Salesforce case.

Figure 7-8 provides an example of how to measure this metric in JIRA for a given month, here October 2020.

("Reporter Team" = Support OR "Reporter Team" = "Client Success") AND created >= 2020-10-01 AND created < 2020-11-01

Figure 7-8. *JIRA query example*

Similarly, the metric could also be retrieved from Salesforce. Figure 7-9 provides an example of how to do this.

Filters	Add ▼						
Show	All cases	▼	Units	Days	▼		
Date Field	Opened Date	▼	Range	Custom	▼	From 5/1/2020	To 4/30/2021

Filter Logic:
(1 AND 2)
1. **Solution Type** not equal to **"Invalid"**
2. **Dev Ticket** not equal to **""**

Figure 7-9. *Salesforce query example*

Note that this Salesforce query measures only valid tickets as the query excludes tickets with the "Solution Type" as "invalid." The query also assumes that development-related tickets are stored in a field called "Dev Ticket."

It might be a good idea to compare the numbers retrieved via these queries to ensure they are the same. If the numbers diverge, support and client success on one side and engineering on the other side measure escalated issues of technical concern differently. A difference in opinion should be avoided, and the queries should get calibrated to measure issues that were captured on behalf of the customer representing technical customer experience issues.

Number of Detected Customer Experience Issues

For engineering organizations actively or even proactively monitoring for customer experience issues in their technical stack that have impact on any of the customer journey paths, it is a good idea to surface the number of issues that were detected and remedied in this way.

While the previously mentioned number of escalated customer experience issues is measuring the fallout of what went wrong and got customer attention, the number of detected customer experience issue metric measures the work of the DCXE and the engineering team in their effort of proactively monitoring, detecting, and mitigating customer experience issues.

Figure 7-10 illustrates how to measure this metric in JIRA as engineers include references to the customer experience issues recorded in their observability tool. The following example assumes the organization uses sessionstack as a customer observability tool. Most observability tools allow sharing of the detected sessions that contain the observed customer experience issue. Take that URL segment and substitute it in the JIRA query example. For FullStory, the string to enter in the query might be "`https://fsty.io/`" as described in the article "Sharing Sessions with Guests" on the FullStory help pages.

> ✓ description ~ "https://app.sessionstack.com/player/" OR comment ~ "https://app.sessionstack.com/player/"   ⑦

Figure 7-10. Customer experience issue query in JIRA

Figure 7-11 shows a graph in a JIRA dashboard tracking the number of detected customer experience issues in an organization that started to proactively identify such issues. Note that this organization carefully selected their observability tool and established a customer observability practice including the designation of engineers as DCXEs.

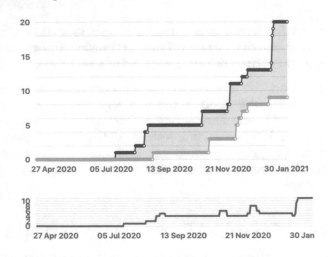

Issues in the last 300 days (grouped daily) View in Issue Navigator
○ Created issues (20)
○ Resolved issues (9)

Figure 7-11. JIRA dashboard tracking number of detected customer experience issues

From the dashboard, you can see how the practice took off as engineers started to raise the issues proactively, discussed the impact with their product owners, and scheduled them to be fixed within their upcoming agile sprints.

At first, the proactively identified numbers might not be large, but they are growing as the observability practice finds more engineers adopting the methods outlined in this book.

Note that each issue proactively identified is an issue prevented from reaching the support or client success organization. It's important to mention this as proactively identified issues are cheaper to fix than issues that were escalated through the support organization or client success organization.

With this said, it might make sense for your organization to compare the number of escalated customer experience issues against the number of proactively detected customer experience issues. The goal should be a graph where the monthly proactively tracked issue amount is hopefully outgrowing the number of escalated issues into the engineering organization. This graph would then express the empathy, care, and focus by engineers toward customer experience issues.

Figure 7-12 provides an example of what this graph could look like. The blue line tracks the number of technical customer experience issues escalated by the support and client success organizations. The orange line tracks the proactively identified and remedied customer experience issues by the engineering team. It illustrates the switch from a reactive to a proactive stance around April of that year. Prior to April, there wasn't a practice of customer experience observability engineering within the engineering team.

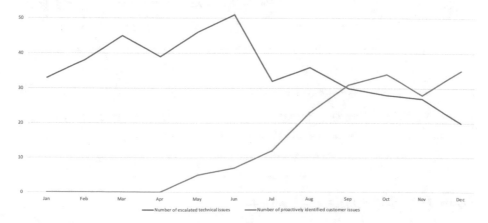

Figure 7-12. Escalated vs. proactively identified customer issues

In and after April, the orange line tracks the issues that were identified and remedied via the observability practice and tools. It shows the increase of adoption. It also shows the inflection point where more issues get proactively identified vs. escalated into the engineering organization. It is clearly visible how such a proactive stance pays off as more customers are satisfied with their experience and are contacting support less about technical issues.

Time to Resolution (TTR) and SLA Adherence

The time to resolution (TTR) metric measures how long it takes from the time a customer experience issue gets brought to the attention of the engineering team, in other words opened, to the time it is resolved. In JIRA, for example, it's the difference between the "Resolved" date and timestamp and the "Created" date and timestamp.

Measuring this metric is especially recommended if there are service-level commitments in play for certain issue severity categories. For example, if priority 1 (P1) level issues are supposed to be resolved within five hours, the ideal TTR is under five hours.

Tracking the average time to resolve per severity or priority level provides an overview of how teams are faring against the SLA commitment.

It might be good to additionally track the SLA adherence level, measuring how many issues stayed within the SLA commitment. Figure 7-13 shows the average time to resolve plotted against the SLA adherence. It is easily visible where the SLA adherence of 100% was met.

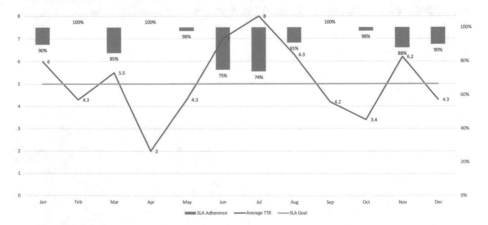

Figure 7-13. Plotting TTR and SLA adherence

In areas where the orange bars appear, the adherence level is not optimal, which means it is coming in at below 100%. The blue line plots the average time to resolution in hours. Note that the SLA for the TTR in this example was five hours. It is now visually easy to see the months that were successful and the months requiring further investigation to understand and counteract trends or to provide help to teams or the system.

Software Security–Related Metrics

In their article "How consumers see cybersecurity and privacy risks and what to do about it," PwC asks a critical question and provides an immediate answer:

> *Can businesses be trusted to secure their customers' personal information? Consumers don't think so.*

They further advise

> *If your customers don't trust you to protect their sensitive data and use it responsibly, you'll get nowhere in your efforts to harness the value of that data to offer a better customer experience.*

It's good to see the correlation between security and customer experience in this sentence. And since there is such a strong correlation, it is recommended to keep an eye on the proactive stance your organization has in addressing software security concerns. Your customers will thank you by feeling more secure when they visit your company's site.

The teams I am working with have experience with SonarQube as a tool providing continuous code inspection, security analysis, and feedback. The tool allows them to fix vulnerabilities prior to becoming a production issue. It also provides a very easy way of reporting on security metrics regarding individual code repositories or on the aggregate level as shown in Figure 7-14.

Figure 7-14. SonarQube security metrics

This figure was retrieved from SonarQube's Security feature description where they explain further:

> Dedicated reports let you track application security against known standard OWASP and SANS categories.

> —SonarQube, *Code Security, For Everyone*

While the preceding metrics provide a good overview on the proactive stance regarding security and the customer experience, the actual number of security incidents should also be tracked.

Since the incidents are always very sensitive, there shouldn't be much detail provided to the larger organization other than the number of security incidents in the live environment. Such a general number provides everybody in the organization a good idea if their proactive stance on preventing security issues actually worked. When it didn't, it helps rally the teams involved in the incident, which they will expediently address. At least, that's my experience each time I was involved in such issues.

Number of Success Criteria Validated

Last, but not least, I am proposing a metric that tracks how teams are caring about the customer experience evaluation at time of release.

We discussed the idea and benefit of success criteria in the section "Implement the Idea of Success Criteria" in Chapter 6. To keep an eye on how many teams are using success criteria in order to improve their quality at the time of release, I am proposing to measure the stories that have success criteria, how many had a positive evaluation of the success criteria, and the number of stories overall.

Figure 7-15 provides a visual overview of such a metric. It also tracks the number of deployments and the number of rollbacks.

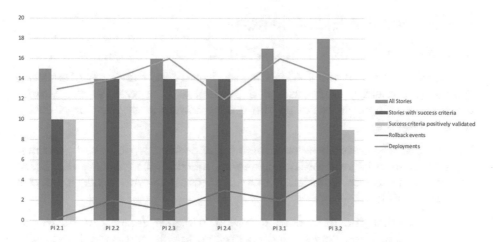

Figure 7-15. Success criteria used as a metric

When the adoption of success criteria is successful, most, if not all, stories will have success criteria. Note that not all success criteria will be "positively validated." Sometimes, teams will measure the success criteria and decide to roll back. This is quite evident in the graph of the example figure marked PI 3.2. In this program increment, there are more rollbacks than usual. Most, but not all, stories have success criteria. Drilling down into the metric should identify the stories that had to be rolled back due to the evaluation of success criteria.

Outside of doing a root cause evaluation, I would encourage you to congratulate the team for rolling back, as they have protected the customer experience and the business by ensuring only verified value gets deployed.

As not all stories are populated with success criteria, it is important to listen to the teams owning the stories and inquiring for why this wasn't set up. Perhaps they didn't have a discussion with the product owner about the business value they should measure, or perhaps they didn't have a way to measure their success criteria for the technical evaluation. Or they did a dark deploy and postpone the success evaluation for when they activate the code with another story. Whatever the reason is, the idea of the metric is to deepen the conversation about release success and to make teams think about measuring and ascertaining their success shortly after release, as nobody likes to roll back later in production with the increased hassle attached to doing so.

A Customer Experience–Centric Quality Dashboard

The section "DevOps and QA" in Chapter 5 discussed the stages of assessing quality (pre-release, at release, and post-release) as well as the various dimensions that could make up the quality components your organization wants to focus on.

This chapter illustrates how to combine the previously discussed customer experience metrics with other engineering metrics into a quality dashboard combining customer experience metrics in context with other important engineering KPIs.

Please note that the dashboard displayed in Figure 7-16 is an illustration created via Excel and PowerPoint. It's created for illustration and discussion purposes only. Keep in mind that it tries to arrange a balance of customer experience metrics in conjunction with other important metrics indicating quality and business success. It's meant as a stimulus for ideation and will hopefully entice you to think how your dashboard should look.

Figure 7-16. Quality dashboard example

Regarding the creation of the dashboard, I do not advise creating such dashboards in Excel and PowerPoint for production use as the creation is time-consuming and periodic updates fraught with high manual effort, delays, and mistakes. Simply put, it doesn't scale this way.

On the other hand, it is valuable to create a mock-up because with a visualized concept it is so much easier to discuss what should go on such a dashboard, how and where the data should be displayed, and what kind of operational elements it should contain.

For example, are red/yellow/green traffic signal style indicators important for visualization or are other visualization methods more effective? How to illustrate the goal attainment and trends per measuring period? What are the measuring periods? Is an always live-updating dashboard desired or should it only contain static data from the last data-pull? These and more are questions that should be answered up front.

Once they are answered, it is much easier to approach a visualization talent in your team with the request to start visualizing in a tool such as Tableau or QuickSight.

For inspiration of styles and ways to visualize the dashboard, I recommend a look at Tableau's business intelligence dashboard examples. Outside of their dashboard examples, they have many more recommendations available on how to do visualizations and also feature fresh and compelling visualizations from the community of users.

Outside of styles, it is of course important to consider that the dashboard doesn't just exist by itself. It relies on a business intelligence infrastructure providing the needed data from the distributed sources of truth. For consideration, please refer to the article "Why you need a BI platform and how to choose one" by Tableau.

The article doesn't necessarily try to convince you to purchase Tableau. It provides awareness for why such a platform needs consideration:

> Business intelligence platforms are more than business analytics software packages. They support your organization's BI strategy by making it easier to access and analyze your data.

—Tableau, "Why you need a BI platform and how to choose one"

And if you are interested in a dashboard utilized by SaaS companies like Walmart Labs or Capital One, I recommend you take a look at Hygieia, another form of a dashboard.

It's a customizable dashboard, and Capital One's case study "How Walmart Scaled Hygieia to 5,000+ Dashboards" illustrates how Walmart Labs implemented Hygieia to automatically track the progress and health of their DevOps teams' activities.

Outside of the need of a data architecture, data lake, a BI platform, and a visualization tool (which could be included in the BI platform), it needs to be clear why there is the need of a dashboard and a customer experience quality strategy. Once this is clear, it should be relatively easy to determine what to track on the dashboard and how to visualize the key metrics.

> *You can't manage what you can't measure.*
>
> —Peter Drucker, Management Consultant

What Peter Drucker meant by this is that you won't know if you are headed in the right direction unless the direction and your success are well defined.

In terms of quality and customer success, you are encouraged to spend time to define success for your organization, to implement the automatic retrieval of the measure points, and to share the picture of customer experience success and quality with your organization via a dashboard.

Useful Tools

The DCXE tool chest

In regard to the role of the DCXE, the tools required for digital customer experience engineering are located at a very specific and interesting intersection. It's the intersection between tools providing observability and analytics in the product area (Product Ops) and tools providing observability within software engineering and operations (DevOps). At this intersection, it is often the DCXE's role to elegantly and effectively link the tools together to provide a quicker path to product insights and issue resolution. We called this work earlier the practice of shifting right (get insight from your customers) and shifting left (find issues quicker at the root of where they occur).

The idea of this tools section is to contribute a view on some tools that enable the DCXE to shift right and then shift left. In other words, enable the DCXE to observe customer friction points and quickly identify the root cause for efficient removal of friction.

As a reminder, the DCXE is active in the space located at the intersection of Product Ops and DevOps (Figure 8-1). The tools used essentially link up the Product Ops space with the DevOps space.

© Lars Wiedenhoefer 2021
L. Wiedenhoefer, *Digital Customer Experience Engineering*,
https://doi.org/10.1007/978-1-4842-7243-5_8

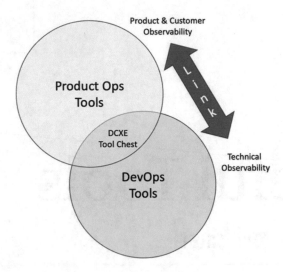

Figure 8-1. Illustration of the Product Ops and DevOps tool space

■ **Reminder** The goals of the DCXE are twofold: (1) to decrease customer experience friction stemming from technical implementations and (2) to accelerate the root cause detection and subsequent resolution of any customer experience friction item.

> *At its core, product ops is the intersection of product (including product design), engineering, and customer success (CS). It exists to support the R&D team and their go-to-market counterparts to improve alignment, communication, and processes around product development, launch, and iteration.*
>
> —Pendo + Product Collective, *The Rise of Product Ops*

As DevOps is the practice of adding IT operations to software development, the addition of Product Ops enables the acceleration of a customer-centric viewpoint of the engineering team. We've seen many examples of this practice in this book.

The space between Product Ops and DevOps is relatively new. Yet, a range of tools already exist and are constantly evolving.

This chapter will discuss several essential tools. Please be aware that this space is rapidly evolving with tool providers expanding their scope, merging with others, and new providers entering the market rapidly. When it comes to tool selection, please take this chapter as a starting point and carefully look at your requirements as well as what's new and how the tools have evolved.

In the following sections, we will be looking at a selection of tools in three separate categories:

- Tools focusing on product analytics

- Tools focusing on customer experience visualization at the session level

- APM tools (measuring friction in the engineering stack and speeding up RCA)

Tools Focusing on Product Analytics

Product analytics tools are essential for getting accurate overviews and insights into the customer experience. These tools illuminate how the customers or certain customer segments navigate through digital experiences, how they engage with digital products and features, and some can even query the customer directly for feedback or even provide guidance.

Figure 8-2 provides an overview of select product analytics tools, each with their unique set of core strengths.

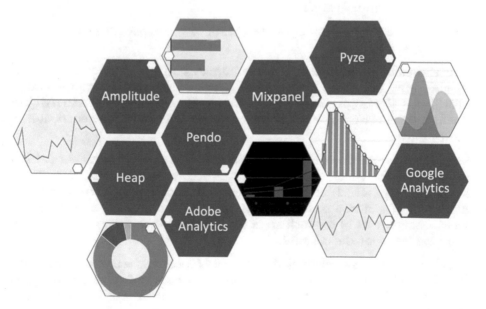

Figure 8-2. Customer journey analytics tools

Let's take a look at some of the key features most of these tools possess:

- Customer experience flow or journey analysis

  See where the customers are going as they enter the digital experience and where they leave.

- Device, platform, and channel analysis

  Understand which devices, operating system, or channel the customer used to get to the experience and while they are on the experience.

- Segmentation and cohort analysis

  Discover how cohorts or segments of your customers are behaving, engaging, and experiencing the digital experience.

- Engagement analysis

  Learn which features are popular vs. which features are ignored or not discovered yet.

- Retention analysis

  Are your customers coming back to the experience and at what rate?

The abovementioned analytical power drives business goals and customer insights on an aggregated level and on a detailed level – to a point. The details provided can be as specific as which buttons the customer clicked to navigate through the experience or how many error events the customer encountered during the flow.

Sometimes, more information is needed to understand the customer session better. A session visualization helps with an accurate replay of the experience leading to insights such as how a specific error impacted the customer or if a placement of a button or feature was perceivable or – going even deeper – which components of the tech stack contributed to the delayed rendering of the experience for the customer.

This level of detail is covered by the next set of tools. These are tools providing high-fidelity insights into the session-level experience while also providing the ability to look under the hood into the tech layer for quicker root cause discovery.

Tools Focusing on Customer Experience Visualization at the Session Level

To clearly see the digital experiences as the customer experienced it is key when it comes to gaining an impression and to being able to empathize with the customer as they may experience friction or conversion issues during their interactions with the digital experience.

Another key need for the DCXE is to be able to correlate the digital experience with the technology stack serving up the experience.

Seeing the experience from the customers' eyes with the ability to look under the hood and link the tech stack to the experience and get started with issue investigations, that's where the tools in Figure 8-3 shine.

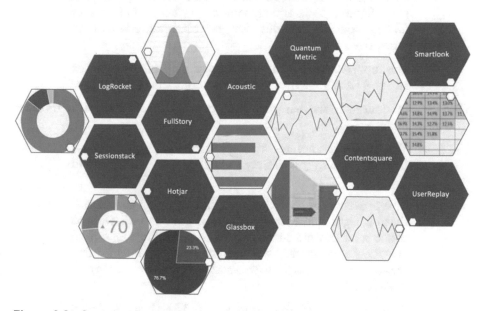

Figure 8-3. Session replay tools

The sample of tools identified here represent the tool chest for the DCXE. It is possible to be a DCXE without them, but the effectiveness of the DCXE is just so much higher when such tools are present. I found in tool evaluation studies that the effectiveness of the software engineering team increased by 30% when working on root cause analysis using the session replay tools' powers.

Key to the efficiency gain is the implementation of the tools combined with the techniques described in Chapter 6.

Typically, the adoption of customer centricity and observability starts with the evaluation of one of the tools illustrated here. Carefully analyze the tools and select the tools providing the feature set most important to your organization.

Some of the key features are

- Instant visual confirmation (a.k.a. session replay) of the customer experience in the same form the customer experienced it, with important enhancements like analytics, developer tools, or friction highlights.

- Heatmaps illustrating where the users interact with the interface.

- Search: Some of the tools allow search by many different predefined criteria already out of the box, which makes finding specific sessions for selected experiences of interest very easy.

- Dashboarding: Create a monitor of the digital experiences and the KPIs your business cares about the most.

There are, of course, more features to discover. The main features of interest to the DCXE are

- The ability to monitor the essential digital experiences (funnels, flows, conversions) via segments, metrics, and events.

- The presence of analytical and dashboarding capabilities that highlight critical insights out of the box vs. having to spend a lot of time searching for them or building out an analytical environment that would present them. In short, out-of-the-box insights, that's the strength of many of these tools.

- As I call it, under the hood views: The ability to "peel back" the surface and look into the tech stack via a JavaScript console or a network view.

- Integrations: The ability to link other tools seamlessly into the session replay tools, which provides even more accelerated insights and quicker root cause discovery.

- Privacy compliance: The ability to mask personally identifiable information (PII) as the intent of watching session replay is about gaining segment and cohort insights without surveillance and other negative connotations. Compliance with any privacy legislation is also top priority, and most, if not all, tools provide answers to this concern.

Keep in mind that the tools listed in Figure 8-3 each have their specific strengths. Again, it's important to evaluate them based on your business needs.

As the session replay tools provide the ability to take a look into the tech stack via tools like consoles or network views, it is not far-fetched to desire a deeper integration that combines session visibility with DevOps-style observability of system properties and patterns. Such integrations are possible by linking APM and error monitoring tools into the customer experience visualization tools. And when these integrations are established, it becomes so much easier to pinpoint technical root causes of customer friction. This is what every DCXE and the engineering teams they are working with desire. It enables them to act quickly on behalf of the customer and allows them to remove friction and be customer centric in their engineering work.

The tools in the next section help with digging deeper into the technology stack, which is absolutely necessary once a session observation discovers that the observed customer friction is of technical nature. Examples here would be an ominous 404 error or other pop-up error messages or even errors that are invisible to the customer but impede the experience.

APM Tools for Measuring Friction in the Engineering Stack and Speeding Up RCA

Let's look at an HTTP status code example. Let's assume the DCXE has set up a monitor tracking the status codes to keep an eye on the impact to the customers.

Figure 8-4 shows an example of how tracking status code errors could look. The example shows a monitored metric named "Sessions with 500 errors."

Sessions with 500 errors

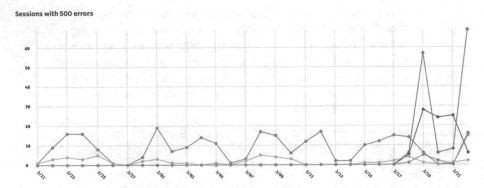

Figure 8-4. A metric tracking 500 error codes in FullStory

The DCXE will notice that there is an unusual spike in a certain experience to the right of the graph on March 19th and then again on March 22nd. Upon watching the session in the session replay tool, the DCXE identifies the exact spot in the session where the 500 error occurs. The network details are illustrated in Figure 8-5.

Figure 8-5. 500 error network details in FullStory

At this point, the DCXE has exhausted the capabilities of the session replay tool and heads over to the application performance management (APM) tool to investigate further. As a refresher, the 500 error is defined as an Internal Server Error. The specific focus of the investigation within the APM tool is now the root cause discovery to identify which server issued the 500 error and why.

Now that we are familiar with the specific use case for digital customer experience engineering, let's look at a set of APM tools that could be of help here. Figure 8-6 provides a set of tools that could be very helpful for the use case identified, namely, to understand and resolve application issues behind the observed customer experience concerns.

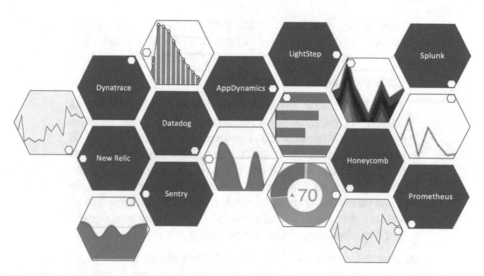

Figure 8-6. APM tool examples

Some of the key features helping the DCXE and the engineering teams looking to quickly resolve the issues or concerns are

- Application monitoring

  This feature provides a clear picture of the application performance health in one view with the ability to drill down into areas of interest. It helps, for example, with finding time-consuming transactions.

- Availability and error monitoring

  When a system is not available or encountering errors, it is most likely not delivering an optimal customer experience. The ability to monitor for high availability and a low error rate is key to working toward a good customer experience.

- Database monitoring

  Monitoring of the database is important when long-running database queries or queries returning with incorrect results are the reason for the customer experience issue.

- In-context observability of metrics, logs, traces, and other application dependencies

This allows the discoverability of issues without further context switching. The idea here is to find any anomaly in the connected and distributed application stack quickly.

- Customer experience and business metrics and analytics

  The APM tools provide an additional set of eyes on the customer experience flow and illustrate the flow in contrast to application performance indicators. It is recommended to link such powerful analytics with the analytics in the tools from the prior sections so that an investigation of customer experience issues can easily traverse across the set of tools from product analytics to session analytics, to application performance analytics, and even back again when needed.

This concludes the overview of the DCXE tool chest. There might be more tools that could be aligned with the tools reviewed here. With the provided overview of the tools in the previous sections, it becomes clear which tools support the DCXE on their quest to reduce customer friction and drive from customer experience metrics to insights and resolution of issues as quickly as possible.

How to Get Started

Today

After now having read most of the book, you have a good idea what it takes to look deeper into customer experience observability in engineering and adjacent functions. So, where will you start?

Start with curiosity, the right mindset, and the right tools. Be curious and have empathy with your customer. Translate this curiosity into the right mindset – a strong belief and certainty that empathy for the customer and their experience can be observed, measured, and improved.

Luckily, the right tools are readily available and can be deployed to fulfill the promise of faster friction discovery, higher customer success and conversion rates, and ultimately increased revenue.

Let's review the starting point of a DCXE and her journey.

Let's call her Jane. Jane joined her team as a software quality assurance engineer. As it is typical for a quality assurance engineer, she was naturally intrigued by defects that were escalated from support and by testing to make

© Lars Wiedenhoefer 2021
L. Wiedenhoefer, *Digital Customer Experience Engineering*,
https://doi.org/10.1007/978-1-4842-7243-5_9

sure less defects were coming back in the future. She was well respected in the team, respected for her product knowledge and insights by the product owner, and on a promotion path in the eyes of her manager.

There was just one thing bothering her. She wasn't happy with her career. She sensed that there was more to customer centricity than testing the product and knowing the product well. She also sensed that the issues coming from the support organization were not going to diminish by better testing. There must be something else. That was the lingering feeling within her.

And then, in the early winter of 2020, several factors came together for her. Outside of working from home due to COVID-19, there was something new going on at her ecommerce SaaS platform company. Her CEO spoke about customer centricity, delighting the customer, speed to market, and building trust. The organization was full of new energy as their market was growing. Additional demand was put on everybody to get the right product to their customers and to ensure that this vital platform was performing well.

As Jane worked in a global company, she knew that keeping up with the growth was vital for the millions of shoppers that depended on her and her colleagues. But how would she know how they were faring? Her team was releasing up to 40 times per sprint with their efficient Continuous Integration/ Continuous Deployment pipeline. Yet, the amount of customer-escalated issues was growing as well.

Her curiosity and passion made her discover a link between the session recording tool the engineers were using for troubleshooting and the product analytics tool the product owner was using. She learned to link the two together, which wasn't hard and could be easily done. The product owner already had mapped the customer journey paths through her application in the product analytics tool. Unfortunately, the twists and turns of this application didn't mean a lot to her unless the customer interaction within a path could be observed. She discovered that the "event" naming in the product analytics tool didn't mean the same as in the language the engineers were using.

After linking up the session recording tool, and observing some interesting customer interactions, she saw a pattern that was concerning. The product analytics tool didn't show the friction as the customers were able to conclude the journey. Jane discovered that the journey was cumbersome and talked to her product owner. Her product owner was highly interested in seeing the customer interactions firsthand. Together, they decided to fix this situation and to make it better. They consulted with the UX team and designed a fix for the new release.

Another remarkable insight came to Jane while she was testing the new fix. She knew she had the measures set up in the product analytics tool, and the session replay tool was linked. The new insight was this: after my testing, I will be able to measure the customer experience once we release the fix to production!

It was this realization that changed her career, and she was on the path to become a digital customer experience engineer.

Jane published an article about her findings and experience and talked to other engineers at the company. At that time, leadership also discussed customer observability while the sales and customer success teams demanded to get more insights into the well-being of their customers during the journey paths through the various products of the platform.

It was the right timing and momentum for her. She discussed her career aspirations and desire to devote more time to customer experience engineering with her director who was championing her career. She advocated for Jane to join a group that had formed. This group was busy discovering many of the items mentioned in this book. Within this group, Jane found purpose, a new grounding in engineering, a new direction in her career, continuous inspiration, an application for her empathy for the customer, her natural curiosity, and her newfound leadership skills.

While this might sound like a fictional story, it is rather not. I know that there are engineers who can relate to Jane's fictional character. Equally relatable is Sorcha McNamee's passage:

> *Observability is something that was new to me in 2020. When I got to grips with customer experience observability, I became really intrigued with just how powerful it could be.*
>
> —Sorcha McNamee, "Piloting FullStory as a
> Customer Experience Observability tool"

In her article on Medium, Sorcha describes how she went through a tool selection to identify the right observability tool; she describes the selection criteria and her findings. And of her results, she says

> *We have seen a reduction in time to insights as well as time to resolution and been able to understand our user friction points all very quickly.*
>
> —Sorcha McNamee, "Piloting FullStory as a
> Customer Experience Observability tool"

I hope that Jane, our fictional DCXE, and Sorcha, our real-world DCXE, are relatable to you and are going to inspire you to invest your curiosity and passion in some of the aspects outlined in this book.

Break It Down into Steps

Rome wasn't built in a day.

—Proverb, *Li Proverbe au Vilain*

When starting with introducing aspects of digital customer experience engineering, start with a foundation. When building such a foundation, identify the aspects within this book that match your business needs.

For example, you have a hunch that there are efficiencies to be gained by introducing a good observability tool into your engineering practice. Creating the foundation, in this case, would be a tool selection and the validation and quantification of that hunch. Once such an evaluation is successful and the tool gets purchased, the next steps are rolling out the tool, teaching the use of the tool, and measuring as well as sharing the benefits of the tool.

In Figure 9-1, the preceding first steps are referred to as the Adopt phase where the engineering teams adopt a customer-centric point of view and practices. This phase is essential and creates the foundation for further growth. Keep in mind that the Adopt phase does not actually end. There are new teams or products to be onboarded. New people will join the organization and need to be introduced to the foundation.

Beyond building and creating the foundation, there is a need to build integrations. The next important phase of building a successful digital customer experience practice within engineering is the Integrate phase.

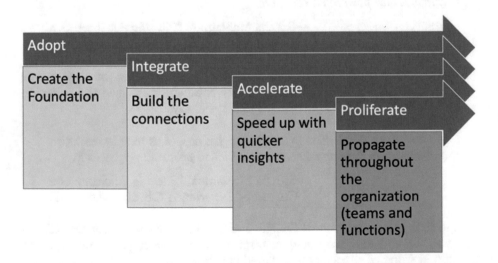

Figure 9-1. Digital customer experience engineering program stages

The Integrate phase looks at the connections that need to be established. These are connections to tools, connections to other teams, as well as connections to knowledge and insights that haven't revealed themselves yet.

Within the Integrate phase, it is advised to further the engineering use cases of detecting and removing customer friction points of technical nature as well as speeding up the root cause analysis. For these use cases, there are already several connections to other tools and practices in need of getting built.

The Integrate phase should also include building connections to other teams and listening to their input and needs. For example, how can the new insights discovered in engineering benefit the product owners or even sales? There might be a new world of information flow or configurations that is yet to be discovered and will benefit the organization in the long run.

Once a sufficient number of integrations have been established, teams will realize efficiencies and productivity improvements. They will discover that they have now reached the Accelerate phase.

In the Accelerate phase, teams focus on benefiting from the new speed, the new normal. For example, discovering the nature of the customer pain, the impact assessment of the escalated pain point, and the root cause all of a sudden don't take as long anymore. Teams are focusing more on creating additional value through new features or new products.

As teams are now realizing the benefit of speed and better customer experience, they talk about the change of the working lifestyle. "Do you remember when it took several days to fix a customer issue and it ruined our sprint and our product owner got angry on behalf of the customer?" And the answer will be: "Luckily these days are in our past."

When other teams hear such conversations or are becoming aware of the benefits of the new customer-focused engineering lifestyle, they want to be included. All of a sudden, the program is not in a push situation anymore where the idea needs to be pushed into the organization. Pulling forces will want to ensure the benefits are reaching all functions and teams within the organization, within and outside of engineering. This phase is called Proliferation phase and the stage is referred to as Proliferate in Figure 9-1. It ensures that all the benefits are propagated and realized throughout the organization.

In the Proliferation phase, your engineering team is already a solid partner of the product organization. Engineering has a valuable seat at the table of the VoC (Voice of the Customer) program. Engineering built out dashboards and information flows to other departments like sales. Engineering and support are working on streamlining the support flow. These are some examples of events that will occur during the Proliferation phase, adding additional benefits to the teams and the business overall.

"So, this will end after a while?" I was asked once. It actually doesn't.

Conceptually, it is a good idea to look at this process in a linear fashion with possibly four stages. It helps with communicating where the organization is at in respect to their maturity. Even in larger organizations that are very mature in the discipline of digital customer experience engineering, the practice is rather a continuum of all the stages (Adopt through Proliferate) at all times. There are new tools or techniques to be discovered, new insights to be analyzed, and new teams and products to be set up.

I've seen organizations where this cycle is ongoing for over 15 years now with ever-increasing business benefits and maturity. They are making the continuous investment into digital customer experience engineering because they know and they measure that this continuous investment is paying off.

Organizational Needs

Most organizations continue to struggle with the complexities and rapidly shifting requirements for delivering an effective, or even average, digital customer experience. The two top-level executives most responsible for this, the CIO and CMO, still have their work cut out to close ranks further and sustainably deliver on what has become the most defining aspect of business today.

—Dion Hinchcliffe, "The evolving role of the CIO and CMO in customer experience"

The challenge Dion points out in his article is to accurately understand where the organization is standing in view of the customer experience. Coming to an accurate and unified view is really key, and it's not only the CIO's responsibility or the CMO's. Arriving at such a unified view is a joint and collaborative responsibility.

To allow the engineering organization within the CIO's remit to grow into this joint responsibility, the organization needs to be set up for success, naturally. Let's discuss what this could look like.

First of all, there needs to be some kind of business case, either obvious or nascent. If a business case for customer experience engineering is not obvious, I encourage you to look closely and investigate. There is enough operational and engineering friction in your organization, any organization, and I am sure you will find it and get inspired, if you look carefully and listen. A quick way to start is just to measure how long it takes to get an average customer escalation of a technical nature detected and resolved. Listen to the customer complaint, analyze how long it took for the team to identify the root cause, find out how long it took to get the issue resolved, and interview people that were involved to identify their friction points. Ask them if they enjoy this type of work. I am very sure they will say that they rather work on feature development than issue fixes. You will get enough responses to identify the business case for your organization.

In the process of inquiry and curiosity, be ready to be met with skepticism and walls. Doors will open, yes, but walls will be built up as well. It's just natural. Run with what you can find out.

During this process, it is very important to look out for a sponsor. You will need someone who has the authority to sponsor the business case and the subsequent work. Now, this is important to remember: if you don't find a sponsor, you will have it much harder and might not succeed. I ran into situations where organizations needed improvement in their digital customer experience, but they didn't want to sponsor the work that was necessary for various reasons that were not obvious. Of course, I also came across more organizations that were very open to engage. Each time this happened, a sponsor appeared, and we moved forward.

If your engineering department is completely new to the approaches outlined in this book, reach out to the other departments that were discussed. Find someone who is interested in CX. You will find them and collaborate with them in one form or another going forward on your journey.

In situations where the engineering department is new to the approaches, start small. Start with a POC and address a portion of the business case you have identified. Show incremental successes and gain a following. And, of course, I say it again, the sponsor.

At this point of time, you will most certainly have found interested parties that are curious and passionate about customer experience. You are working with them on initiatives, but it's not their full-time job to devote all their time to the effort. That's okay. It's most likely not your full-time job either.

It's the passionate efforts that build toward something incrementally that create a successful network and team.

Ultimately, when digital customer experience engineering and the customer observability practice gets adopted and it grows, it is smart to have a small group of dedicated people devoted to serving the organization. Luckily, this doesn't have to be a large team. I've worked at large multinationals that scaled customer experience engineering globally where the core team working on this was three to four people strong.

Figure 9-2 provides an example of an organizational setup. Note the top role of the sponsor. In my current organization, we have a VP who is sponsoring the effort and helps with strategic alignment and the removal of roadblocks. The sponsor also will help with alignment of the effort to the company goals. Remember, it's important to even get your CEO to support your efforts. It's that important!

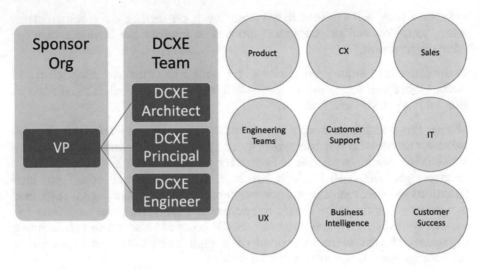

Figure 9-2. Organizational setup example

Our core team started out with a customer experience engineering strategist or architect. We arranged engineers around this role to move the initiative from infancy to a critical point where we had the practice firmly adopted in key teams with enough practitioners, success artifacts, and training materials in place for others to follow.

This concluded for us the first phase of the Adopt stage. We then formed a group around going through the Integrate, Accelerate, and Proliferate stages. You will need engineers to build out the integration pieces that are technical in nature. They will manage the tools and integrations. They will help with collecting the business intelligence data to prove your business case and paint the picture of success. The engineers will also help curate the data to ensure there's no mess accumulated, which can quickly happen. They are also going to ensure the privacy principles are implemented correctly. You will need possibly one or two, depending on your scale and setup. And you will need a passionate evangelist on your team. Someone who is going through the organization working with and educating others, teaching them how to find the customer friction and to train the trainers who will train others in the subject.

Your team will become an integral part of any Voice of the Customer effort and CX initiative. You will thrive, your team will thrive, the organization will thrive, and your customers will thank you for it.

So, be curious, passionate, have empathy for your customers and a zest for customer experience excellence. It will benefit your customers, the organization, and your career. You will feel good doing the right thing, every day.

I

Index

© Lars Wiedenhoefer 2021
L. Wiedenhoefer, *Digital Customer Experience Engineering*,
https://doi.org/10.1007/978-1-4842-7243-5

Printed in the United States
by Baker & Taylor Publisher Services